guidebooks have unlocked the secrets
of destinations around the world,
sharing with travellers a wealth of
experience and a passion for travel.

**Rely on Thomas Cook as your
travelling companion on your next trip
and benefit from our unique heritage.**

Thomas Cook **pocket** guides

PARIS

Garry Marchant &
Marnie Mitchell

Written by Garry Marchant & Marnie Mitchell, updated by Mike Gerrard
Original photography by Garry Marchant

Published by Thomas Cook Publishing
A division of Thomas Cook Tour Operations Limited
Company registration no. 3772199 England
The Thomas Cook Business Park, Unit 9, Coningsby Road,
Peterborough PE3 8SB, United Kingdom
Email: books@thomascook.com, Tel: +44 (0) 1733 416477
www.thomascookpublishing.com

Produced by Cambridge Publishing Management Limited
Burr Elm Court, Main Street, Caldecote CB23 7NU
www.cambridgepm.co.uk

ISBN: 978-1-84848-548-8

© 2006, 2008, 2010 Thomas Cook Publishing
This fourth edition © 2012
Text © Thomas Cook Publishing
Maps © Thomas Cook Publishing/PCGraphics (UK) Limited
Transport map © Communicarta Limited

Project Editor: Karen Beaulah
Production/DTP: Steven Collins

Printed and bound in Spain by GraphyCems

Cover photography © Gavin Hellier

CONTENTS

INTRODUCING PARIS

Introduction......................................6
When to go 8
Paris: seriously romantic 12
History...14
Lifestyle..16
Culture...18

MAKING THE MOST OF PARIS

Shopping..22
Eating & drinking.....................24
Entertainment & nightlife.....28
Sport & relaxation 32
Accommodation 34
The best of Paris......................40
Suggested itineraries 42
Something for nothing...........44
When it rains 46
On arrival.....................................48

THE CITY OF PARIS

Right Bank West 62
Right Bank East...........................80
Left Bank......................................98

OUT OF TOWN TRIPS

Auvers-sur-Oise 122
Reims 128

PRACTICAL INFORMATION

Directory 140
Emergencies 154

INDEX 156

MAPS

Paris 50
Paris transport map 54
Right Bank West 63
Right Bank East..........................81
Left Bank......................................99
Auvers-sur-Oise 123
Reims 129

SYMBOLS KEY

The following symbols are used throughout this book:

@ address ☎ telephone ⓦ website address ⓛ opening times
ⓝ public transport connections ❶ important

The following symbols are used on the maps:

𝑖	information office	■	point of interest
✈	airport		
✚	hospital		
🛡	police station		
⊟	bus station		
⊒	railway station		
Ⓜ	metro		
✝	cathedral		
❶	numbers denote featured cafés & restaurants		

Hotels and restaurants are graded by approximate price as follows:
£ budget price ££ mid-range price £££ expensive

Abbreviations used in addresses:

av.	avenue
blvd	boulevard
pl.	place (square)

▶ *The Arc de Triomphe: Napoleon's victories set in stone*

INTRODUCING
Paris

London Borough of Southwark	
D	
SK 1872736 0	
Askews & Holts	08-Jun-2012
914.436 MAR TRAV	£5.99

Introduction

The key to Paris's immense attractiveness – and it's the most popular tourist destination on the planet – is its charisma: it knows that, even after all these years, it still sets the standard.

With an almost magnetic beauty, Paris's visual appeal makes it easily the world's most gorgeous city. In the space of a few miles you'll find tree-lined boulevards such as the Champs-Élysées and Saint-Germain, and magnificent monuments such as the Arc de Triomphe, the Louvre and Notre-Dame. Even the Town Hall, the Hôtel de Ville, is a work of art. And then there are the bridges, the fountains and the Seine itself.

Yet the city has more to offer than good looks; indeed, Paris's record of cultural achievement makes superlatives inevitable. Year after year, it presents the world with the most intriguing museums, the most exciting sense of fashion, the most progressive artistic innovations and, of course, the most ravishing food and drink.

The long-established human iconography of the city – cancan dancers at the Moulin Rouge, accordion players in the metro, booksellers along the Seine – exists in real life to this day, and with a sense of style that prevents any chance of a descent into cliché. Paris isn't self-satisfied, stodgy or staid; it's vibrant, vital and quirky. This is, after all, the city that has the panache to build its own temporary beach once a year so that the people who live and work here can go on holiday every lunchtime; this is the city that has enough sense of fun to turn itself into a giant rollerblading circuit every Friday night when thousands of skaters whizz through its cobbled streets and gigantic thoroughfares; this is the city that sprays perfume all over its underground system in the morning because it allows its homeless to sleep there at night.

Living is considered an art form here, and every reaction to the experience of life is given stylish expression. Religion is practised and celebrated with gusto; so is love, so is art and so are bawdiness and sleaze.

It's so easy to take it all for granted, but imagine what the world would be like without Paris. If the city didn't exist, we'd simply have to invent it. Thankfully, the French already have, and you really should come and make the most of the huge favour they've done the rest of us.

⬢ *You're never far from a fantastic choice of food throughout the city*

When to go

Paris is an unsurpassable destination at any time of the year. Summer favours strolling in parks and boulevards, taking a trip on the Seine or spending hours sitting outside a café. Winters are great for investigating the city's cultural and entertainment venues – and for spending hours sitting *inside* a café.

SEASONS & CLIMATE

While Paris is at its most beautiful in spring and autumn, it is worth visiting at any time. Summer can be hot, but it is generally pleasant, with more hours of daylight. In August, quite a few Parisians leave the city for their annual holiday, so many non-central restaurants, cafés and small businesses close.

Tourists descend on the city year-round, but particularly in July and August, so queues at museums and other attractions can be long. During autumn, parks, gardens and tree-lined boulevards are awash with rich colours, and leaves pattern the ground as days get shorter and cooler.

Paris may see the occasional grey day in autumn and winter, but temperatures are rarely extreme.

ANNUAL EVENTS

There is always something going on in Paris, more than even a resident could ever hope to attend. For the latest information on events, see Ⓦ www.parisinfo.com

January & February

Paris-wide sales last from mid-January to late February. Parisians' sales protocol is considerably less feral than that of their Anglo-Saxon neighbours.

April

Grandes Eaux Musicales (musical fountain displays) Performed
on Saturdays, Sundays and some public holidays from April to
the end of October and Tuesdays from mid-May to the end of
June. ⓐ Parc du Château de Versailles, Versailles ❶ Bookings: 01 30 83
78 89 ⓦ www.chateauversailles-spectacles.fr or
www.chateauversailles.fr Ⓜ RER: Versailles-Rive Gauche

Marathon de Paris A 42-km (26-mile) race through Paris, starting
at the Champs-Élysées (8th). ⓦ www.parismarathon.com

   If this is too much to start with, try the Semi Marathon de Paris
21 km (13 miles) in March. If that's too much, simply spectate.

May

French Open Tennis Championships This event is both a grand-
slammer in its own right and a great gauge for seeing who's on form
for Wimbledon. ⓐ Stade Roland-Garros, 2 av. Gordon-Bennett, 16th
❶ 08 26 65 00 00 ⓦ www.rolandgarros.com Ⓜ Metro: Porte d'Auteuil

Musique Côté Jardins Music is performed in the city's parks and
gardens from May to September. ⓦ www.jardins.paris.fr

June–August

Le Cinéma en Plein Air (mid-June–mid-July) A massive screen is
set up in the park and, for more than one month, you can settle in
a deckchair and watch evening showings of classic films for free.
ⓐ Parc de la Villette, 19th ⓦ www.villette.com

Fête de la Musique On 21 June Paris joins the rest of France in
celebrating music, at a festival which began in France, but has now
spread throughout the rest of the world as World Music Day. Look
for street performers and free concerts throughout the city.
ⓦ www.fetedelamusique.culture.fr

Paris Jazz Festival The best jazz sounds are played from early June to the end of July. ❸ Parc Floral de Paris, 12th ❶ 01 49 57 24 84 Ⓦ www.parcfloraldeparis.com

Bastille Day (14 July) Celebrate France's national holiday with a military parade down the Champs-Élysées with jets swooping overhead and fireworks over the Eiffel Tower in the evening.

Festival Chopin A celebration of the semi-French composer begins in mid-June and lasts for a month. ❶ 01 45 00 22 19 Ⓦ www.frederic-chopin.com

Finale of the Tour de France (late July) The final stage of the world's most exacting cycle race never fails to excite extreme emotions. ❸ av. des Champs-Élysées, 8th Ⓦ www.letour.fr

Paris-Plage (mid-July–mid-August) Quays on both banks of the Seine in the city centre are transformed into a beach, with music, food, sand and palm trees, boules and a general party atmosphere. Following the success of this trend-setting event, cities from Berlin to Rome have created their own versions. ❶ 39 75 within France Ⓦ www.paris.fr

Quartier d'Été Festival (Summer Festival) Music, films and other happenings throughout Paris from mid-July to early August. ❶ 01 44 94 98 00 Ⓦ www.quartierdete.com

Nocturnes Splendid sound and light show with perfume and fireworks on Saturday evenings from mid-June to the end of August at the château's Bassin de Neptune. ❸ Parc du Château de Versailles ❶ 01 30 83 78 89 Ⓦ www.chateauversailles-spectacles.fr

Late August–September

Jazz at La Villette Top names and new artists converge at the Parc de la Villette for this music shindig from the end of August to mid-September. ❸ Parc de la Villette, 19th ❶ 01 40 03 75 75 Ⓦ www.villette.com

Festival d'Automne à Paris (Paris Autumn Festival) This celebrates autumnal events from mid-September to the end of December. ☎ 01 53 45 17 00 Ⓦ www.festival-automne.com

Journées du Patrimoine Normally off-limits buildings such as the Palais de l'Élysée, the President's residence, are opened to the public for the third weekend in September. Ⓦ www.journeesdupatrimoine.culture.fr

October

Nuit Blanche All night you can visit the normally hidden side of nocturnal Paris, revealed through performances, monument visits and installations. ☎ 39 75 (within France) Ⓦ www.paris.fr

---

PUBLIC HOLIDAYS

New Year's Day 1 Jan
Easter Monday 9 Apr 2012, 1 Apr 2013, 21 Apr 2014
May Day 1 May
Victory Day, WW II 8 May
Ascension 17 May 2012, 9 May 2013, 29 May 2014
Bastille Day 14 July
Assumption of the Virgin Mary 15 Aug
All Saints Day 1 Nov
1918 Armistice Day 11 Nov
Christmas Day 25 Dec

On public holidays expect almost all shops and many restaurants to be closed. If a holiday falls on a Tuesday or Thursday, many Parisians like to *faire le pont* and take the Monday or Friday off too.

Paris: seriously romantic

The marketing of major cities as tourist destinations has long relied on clichés to identify individual brands. Thus New York is a big apple that's so good they named it twice; Copenhagen is wonderful, wonderful; and Rome, Venice and Adelaide are all the one and only City of Light.

And Paris? Is it really, as we are so often told, the city of romance?

Well, it's certainly heaving with amorous couples, romantic alleys and dreamy squares, chief among which is the glorious Place des Vosges in the Marais (see page 44). From the moment this perfectly symmetrical square was completed in 1612, it became a location for romantic couplings, not least thanks to the huge contribution made by its most famous early resident, the prolific courtesan Marion Delorme. Even now, it's a prime spot for romantic strolls and intimate picnics. So, yes, Paris is romantic, but its residents are hardly coy. André Malraux, the leading French cultural figure of the last century, called the beautiful triangular garden of **Place Delphine** (🚇 Île de la Cité, 1st Ⓜ Metro: Cité) 'undoubtedly Paris's vagina'. This was meant as a compliment.

Paris not only deserves its reputation as being literally romantic; it has an irrefutable claim to being literarily Romantic, which is how it acquired its reputation for inspiring a kind of dark and brooding passion (see Paris in the Movies, pages 58–9). The Romantic writers of the 18th century took the Renaissance identification of genius with melancholy a step further by equating it with early death. An international style of conspicuous suffering became popular, and the 1830s saw a rash of 'Suicide Clubs' forming throughout the city. Their members took to hurling themselves into the Seine with such enthusiasm that the clubs were banned. Although this is an idea that today seems risible to all but the most vapid emo who's been plunged into morbid depression by the side effects of his acne medication, Paris has been the site of some iconic premature departures: Oscar Wilde, Jim Morrison and Princess Diana all checked out rather too early here.

Should either the hearts-and-flowers or the deep-and-meaningful facets of Paris's romantic appeal move you to the kind of gesture that can only be made on one knee, another charming square, **Place Vendôme** (🅰 1st 🅜 Metro: Tuileries) is full of expensive jewellery shops.

⬥ *Paris as in the movies...*

History

The French capital began its life as a modest fishing village on a small island (now the Île de la Cité) in the Seine. Around 225 BC, a Gallic tribe, the Parisii, inhabited it, but when Caesar's legions invaded 200 years later, they set fire to their tiny settlement and fled. The Romans subsequently expanded and developed the village, which was just an anonymous outpost of their empire, changing its name first to Lutetia, and then finally to Paris.

It was Clovis the Franc who first raised Paris's profile by making it the capital of his kingdom in 470. The city rapidly became a centre of Christianity and remained relatively stable, despite the attentions of the Vikings. The 13th-century reign of Philippe Auguste saw it modernise and expand again; the early Middle Ages were a golden time that only came to an end when Paris was devastated by Black Death. In the late 16th century, Henri of Navarre rebuilt the capital and, by the time Louis XIV (the 'Sun King') came to the throne a century later, it was re-established as an important and sophisticated city. The two subsequent kings Louis enjoyed their power rather too much, though: during the French Revolution, Paris was at the centre of events, with the storming of the Bastille prison and much blood shed on its streets, especially via the guillotine in what is now called Place de la Concorde.

Republican Paris developed steadily through the Industrial Revolution, the French Second Empire, and the belle époque. The architectural style by which we identify the city today was established when Napoleon III commissioned Baron Haussmann to transform it into a glorious, 19th-century capital. The Baron largely created the shape of modern Paris, with its broad boulevards and distinctive buildings.

In the 19th and 20th centuries, Paris was enduring the ravages of wars at the same time as it was establishing itself as a centre of artistic achievement and the spicier types of leisure pursuit. Times could be exceedingly hard for Parisians: during the Franco-Prussian War siege, for example, starvation forced them to eat the zoo animals. The city's lowest point in modern history came during World War II, when German troops occupied it for four years.

Charles de Gaulle was the dominant figure in post-World War II France. By May 1968, however, the country had had enough of his system of government (the 'Fifth Republic', which was basically an elected monarchy), and students on Paris's Left Bank started an uprising that eventually led to his downfall. After the uneventful presidencies of Pompidou and Giscard d'Estaing, Mitterrand revived the notion of President as monarch and left behind such monuments to his rule as the Louvre's pyramid and the Opéra Bastille.

His successor, Jacques Chirac, also conducted himself as an autocrat and, although Paris briefly became the focus of the world's attention when Princess Diana was killed in a car crash here in 1997, it is the reaction to Chirac's presidency that has had the largest impact on the feeling of the modern city. While the country as a whole saw a shift to the far right, Paris's impulse was to elect the left-winger Bertrand Delanoë as its Mayor; Delanoë has had a huge impact on the city. Chirac has gone, having been replaced by Nicolas Sarkozy in May 2007, but Delanoë continues as Mayor and has recently unveiled his 'Plan Local d'Urbanisme', a vision of Paris's future that places the income generated by tourism at the heart of the city's economic prosperity. Visitors, then, should look forward to seeing even greater improvements in this great city in the future, as Paris heads confidently forward.

Lifestyle

For all its world-renowned monuments, Paris is not a museum but a living city. Place du Palais Royal, across from the Louvre, is often buzzing with activity, whether it's skateboarders weaving around coloured cones, rap or rock musicians jamming, or a farmers' market selling *pain de campagne* (rustic bread) or *saucisson* (sausage). In many neighbourhoods, food markets are held on weekends, when Parisians patronise their local stalls. (See Ⓦ www.paris.fr for the market list.)

Parisians love to gather at cafés, squares and along the quays and pedestrian bridges (such as the Pont des Arts), whenever time and weather permit. To return central Paris to the people, the Town Hall closes the Seine-side roads to traffic and opens them to pedestrians on Sundays and public holidays. The result is a huge success, with strollers, cyclists and skaters taking over the riverbanks. On Sundays along the newly popular Canal Saint-Martin in the 10th *arrondissement*, the Quai de Valmy and Quai de Jemmapes are also turned over to pedestrians. Place de l'Hôtel de Ville, in front of the Town Hall, throbs with activity year-round. In summer, sand and palm trees are transported here for public volleyball courts during the hugely successful Paris-Plage (see page 10) when the quays of the centre are turned into a riverside 'beach'. In the winter, the square transforms into an ice rink, with free skate hire and festive music.

On fine days, Parisians can be seen walking their dogs or occupying every inch of space on lawns and metal chairs in such parks as the Jardin du Luxembourg (see page 100) and the Jardin des Tuileries (see page 64). Whatever the weather, locals love getting together with family and friends, and young people and couples linger for hours at street cafés, mobile phones in one hand, cigarettes in another. However, since 1 January 2008, it is illegal to smoke in all public places, a legislative development that severely tests the rebellious Parisian psyche.

🔺 *Strolling towards Place de la Concorde*

Culture

Paris defines the notion of a cultural city. It has always been a centre of architectural innovation: both the Eiffel Tower and I M Pei's *Pyramid* at the Louvre, sparked controversy when first built, yet today they are heralded as marvels of cutting-edge design.

Though it was first developed some 35 years ago, the Centre Pompidou (see page 86), which houses the Museum of Modern Art, is still considered revolutionary, which is far from a pejorative term in the local context. Despite the view of some Parisians that the chunky exterior pipes are worthy of a plumber's nightmare, the building is a success for its museum space and panoramic views across Paris.

Another example of original design stands near the Eiffel Tower. The Musée du Quai Branly (see page 111), designed by Jean Nouvel and opened in 2006, has a principal façade that follows the curve of the Seine, as well as a 'living culture' space for theatre, music and dance. However, its 'green wall', which was such a startling feature of its design when it opened, has proved to be problematic. When the plants die off in winter, it causes frost damage to the innovative building.

As one of the world's cultural capitals, Paris always has exhibitions of such great artists as Ingres, Chagall and Monet; but springing up in the northern Marais neighbourhood is a wonderful collection of small, unpretentious, designer boutiques and art galleries. Among the fashion designers are **Gaspard Yurkievich** (❷ 43 rue Charlot) and **Shine** (❷ 15 rue de Poitou); for contemporary art galleries stroll down Rue Charlot to find **Chantal Crousel** (❶ 01 42 77 38 87 ❿ www.crousel.com), **Denise René** (❶ 01 48 87 73 94) and **Frédéric Giroux** (❶ 01 42 71 01 02 ❿ www.fredericgiroux.com).

Even for locals, the choice in Paris can be overwhelming, with some 1,800 classified monuments, 140 museums and 145 theatres.

⬣ *The Viaduc des Arts (see page 93)*

The weekly publication *Pariscope* has complete event listings, with around 50 pages dedicated to theatres alone.

The city's museums range from the great, such as the Louvre (see pages 70–71) and the Musée d'Orsay (see pages 109–11), to the offbeat, such as the **Musée de l'Erotisme** (❷ 72 blvd de Clichy, 18th ❶ 01 42 58 28 73 ❿ www.musee-erotisme.com) and the **Musée de la Contrefaçon** (❷ 16 rue de la Faisanderie, 16th ❶ 01 56 26 14 03), showcasing counterfeits of all types. Almost all museums charge an admission fee. For details on exemptions and free-entry times and days, see page 44.

The two opera houses, the majestic Palais Garnier (see pages 72–3) with its gold-leaf embellishments and the modern glass-fronted Opéra Bastille (see page 90), opened for the bicentennial of the French Revolution, provide a full and varied programme of opera and ballet throughout the year (except August, when Paris goes on holiday). In an effort to attract a broader (and younger) audience to opera and ballet performances, the Opéra Bastille offers standing places for just €5, available from an hour and a half before the start of the performance. A similar system operates at the Palais Garnier, although tickets there sometimes cost €10. Under-28s can also purchase any unsold tickets at low rates (€10–25) just before the start of the show.

Performing arts venues range from the mega, such as the **Palais des Congrès** (❷ 2 pl. de la Porte Maillot, 17th ❶ 01 40 68 28 00), to the mini of the cloakroom-sized cabarets and theatres in Montmartre.

Even the quality of the busker is higher in Paris than in many cities, with some highly talented artistes adorning the city's streets and metro stations.

❶ *Just one of the city's spectacular views*

MAKING THE MOST OF
Paris

Shopping

Paris is the epicentre of haute couture, with all the top names occupying select addresses along the exclusive Avenue Montaigne, Champs-Élysées, Rue du Faubourg Saint-Honoré, Place Vendôme and Rue Royale. Even if you can only afford to window-shop, it is fun to stroll past such bastions of high fashion as Cartier, Chanel, Louis Vuitton, Gucci, Dior, Lalique, Longchamps, Hermès, Christian Lacroix, Jean-Paul Gaultier and Versace. There is even a list of officially sanctioned haute-couture houses at ⓦ www.modeaparis.com

You can get a cross-section of goods in the city's excellent department stores, such as Galeries Lafayette (see pages 75–6) and Le Printemps (see page 76) on Boulevard Haussmann in the 9th *arrondissement*, Le Bon Marché (see page 112), with its famous food store, in the 7th, and the **BHV** (ⓐ 52 rue de Rivoli, 4th ⓞ 01 42 74 90 00 ⓦ www.bhv.fr), across from the Hôtel de Ville in the 4th. All have the latest in ready-to-wear fashions as well as household items.

One of the biggest shopping centres is the **Forum des Halles** (ⓐ 101 Porte Berger ⓞ 01 44 76 96 56 ⓦ www.forumdeshalles.com ⓛ 10.00–20.00 Mon–Sat), a mostly underground mall that is huge and can be confusing. Some find it soulless, but it is always packed with Parisians browsing the mainly chain stores that cover fashion, music, food and drink, jewellery, toys and homewares.

The Marais, the city's oldest district, where ancient buildings lean into cobbled streets, has an eclectic variety of little boutiques. Other fun shops here include stationery stores and a wealth of food shops, including some wonderfully wicked patisseries. Although Sunday shopping is largely prohibited except at Christmas time and during the sales (January, February and June), it carries on in the Marais (mainly in the 4th). On sombre Sundays, busy shops add animation to

USEFUL SHOPPING PHRASES

What time do the shops open/close?
A quelle heure ouvrent/ferment les magasins?
Ah kehlur oovr/fehrm leh mahgazhang?

How much is this?
C'est combien?
Seh combyahng?

Can I try this on?
Puis-je essayer ceci?
Pweezh ehssayeh cerssee?

My size is ...
Ma taille (clothes)/
Ma pointure (shoes) est ...
*Mah tie/mah
pooahngtewr ay ...*

I'll take this one, thank you
Je prends celui-ci/
celle-ci, merci
*Zher prahng serlweesi/
sehlsee, mehrsee*

such streets as Francs Bourgeois, and trendy boutiques around the quays Valmy and Jemmapes and their side streets in the Canal Saint-Martin district in the 10th *arrondissement* are also open.

Across the river on the Left Bank, Boulevard Saint-Germain is the thoroughfare to shop, sip coffee, stroll and people-watch. As well as the boulevard, its side streets, Rue du Four and Rue des Saints-Pères, and the streets around Saint-Sulpice church, are full of little boutiques selling such items as daring lingerie and funky embroidered bags.

Also not to be missed are the city's many markets, specialising in everything from farm-produced cheeses to *grand-mère*'s antiques.

For a stylish memento of your stay, the museum boutiques, selling art cards, prints and classy trinkets, are worth a browse.

Eating & drinking

As a world culinary capital, Paris has an impressive variety of restaurants, brasseries and bistros. With 10,000 bars and restaurants, the only problem you'll have is choosing where to go. Dedicated gourmets can dine at the crème de la crème, the chefs' restaurants such as **Fogón** (Spanish cuisine) (🄰 45 quai des Grands Augustins, 6th ❶ 01 43 54 31 33 🖤 www.fogon.fr Ⓜ Metro: Saint-Michel) and **Chez l'Ami Jean** (Basque cuisine) (🄰 27 rue Malar, 7th ❶ 01 47 05 86 89 🖤 www.amijean.eu Ⓜ Metro: Invalides). Other top dining experiences can be had at the Michelin-starred **La Tour d'Argent** (🄰 15–17 quai de la Tournelle, 5th ❶ 01 43 54 23 31 🖤 www.tourdargent.com Ⓜ Metro: Cardinal Lemoine) and the Philippe Starck-designed **Kong** (🄰 1 rue du Pont Neuf, 1st ❶ 01 40 39 09 00 🖤 www.kong.fr Ⓜ Metro: Pont Neuf), where views are superb and lofty, and prices are pretty rarefied too ❶ Reservations are essential at each of these restaurants

A recent trend has seen renowned chefs opening small *prix d'amis* (affordable price) restaurants in order to bring fine food to a wider group of discerning diners: Alain Senderens renounced his three Michelin stars to set up the unpretentious **Senderens** (🄰 9 pl. de la Madeleine, 8th ❶ 01 42 65 22 90 🖤 www.senderens.fr); Pierre Gagnaire opened the **Gaya** (🄰 44 rue du Bac, 7th ❶ 01 45 44 73 73) and others are following suit.

PRICE CATEGORIES

Restaurant ratings in this book are based on the average price of a three-course dinner without drinks:

£ up to €45   ££ €45–60   £££ over €60

For those on a budget, many restaurants serve set meals of several courses, with *entrée* and *plat* (main course), or *plat* and *dessert*, or all three for a fixed price. Bistros offer home-style cooking in an informal atmosphere, while brasseries provide sandwiches, salads or simple meals most of the day. Wine bars have quality wines with tasty snacks or meals to accompany them.

Too many simple restaurants and brasseries, especially in tourist areas, limit their menus to roast chicken or steak and chips. If you'd like something other than chips, they may provide a salad or vegetables instead. Despite their modest surroundings and prices, many brasseries and bistros serve fresh market produce.

The greatest collection of budget restaurants is in the popular and touristy Saint-Michel area in the Latin Quarter. The warren of cobbled streets near Place Saint-Michel, especially on rues de la Huchette, de la Harpe and Saint-Séverin, is crammed with restaurants and bars.

The Montmartre area is known for its African restaurants, serving such dishes as *mafé* (West African meat in peanut sauce) and *yassa* (Senegalese chicken, mutton or fish in a lemon, mustard and onion sauce). Chinese fare is authentic and plentiful in the 13th *arrondissement*, Japanese along Rue Sainte-Anne in the 2nd, while

⏷ *A restaurant on the Left Bank*

Indian restaurants can be found in Passage Brady in the 10th. *Traiteurs* (takeaways), especially Chinese, serve budget meals and sometimes you can eat on the premises. They are simple, but good value. (For more info on ethnic food, see Multicultural Paris, pages 118–19.)

French fare changes with the seasons. In autumn and winter, fishmongers set up stalls in front of many brasseries and serve fresh oysters. During cold months, hearty, warming cheese dishes from the mountain region of the Savoy – fondues, raclettes and *tartiflettes* – are popular. In summer, fresh fruits and vegetables are plentiful in markets and on menus and Parisians love dining alfresco late into the evening.

For ordinary brasseries and simple restaurants there is usually no need to book a table in advance, unless you are a large group or intend to go on a Friday or Saturday evening. More time should be allowed for reserving at haute-cuisine restaurants, which often need to be booked weeks in advance and confirmed the day before. At the more exclusive restaurants, men should wear a jacket and tie, especially in the evenings. Otherwise, the dress code is fairly relaxed. Many restaurants are closed on Sunday, but the local weekly listings publication, *Pariscope*, lists some venues that are open (*ouvert le dimanche*).

Few of France's top restaurants and traditional brasseries are vegetarian-friendly, though some simple cafés, takeaways and lunch

GALETTE DES ROIS

If you're in Paris in January, try a *galette des Rois* – a round almond-based pie sometimes flavoured with raspberry or pistachio. Look out for the *fève* (lucky charm) in your slice. Although traditionally eaten at Epiphany, *boulangeries* sell them throughout January.

counters are starting to serve *bio* (organic) fare. One, started by two chefs and known for its quality, is **Eatme** (✉ 38 rue Léopold Bellan, 2nd ☎ 01 42 36 18 28).

USEFUL DINING PHRASES

I would like a table for two/three/four people
Je voudrais une table pour deux/trois/quatre personnes
Zher voodray oon tabl poor dur/trwah/kahtr pehrson

Waiter/Waitress!
Monsieur/Mademoiselle,
s'il vous plaît!
M'sewr/madmwahzel, sylvooplay!

May I have the bill, please?
L'addition, s'il vous plaît!
Laddyssyawng, sylvooplay!

Could I have it well cooked/medium/rare, please?
Je le voudrais bien cuit/à point/saignant, s'il vous plaît
Zher ler voodray beeang kwee/ah pwang/saynyang, sylvooplay

I am a vegetarian. Does this contain meat?
Je suis végétarien (végétarienne).
Est-ce que ce plat contient de la viande?
Zher swee vehzhehtarianhg (vehzhehtarien).
Essker ser plah kontyang der lah veeahngd?

Where is the toilet (restroom), please?
Où sont les toilettes, s'il vous plaît?
Oo sawng leh twahlaitt, sylvooplay?

Entertainment & nightlife

From all-night discos to cosy wine bars and what some euphemistically call 'naughty Paris', the city truly has something for every nightlife temperament. To find out what's on during your stay, see the English-language Ⓦ www.parisnightlife.fr

The long summer nights give Parisians several more hours of daylight after their work day, when they can dine or drink at outdoor restaurants and bars. Free summer concerts fill the parks and gardens from May to September, while festivals and music *fêtes* fill the streets and bars with a lively, late-night atmosphere during sultry months.

Trendy clubs include Rex Club (see page 79) and **Le Social Club** (Ⓐ 142 rue Montmartre Ⓦ www.parissocialclub.com) in the 2nd *arrondissement*, or **Le Nouveau Casino** (Ⓦ www.nouveaucasino.net) in the hip nightlife district of Rue Oberkampf in the 11th. The Bastille district (also in the 11th) is ever-popular thanks to its party atmosphere, bistros, clubs and bars.

The river after dark is as bright with action as it is with lights, aided by such floating clubs as Le Batofar (see page 117) and **La Dame de Canton** (Ⓐ River Seine, in front of Bibliothèque François Mitterrand Ⓦ www.damedecanton.com Ⓜ Quai de la Gare) in the 13th *arrondissement* and the Bâteau Six-Huit on Quai de Montebello in the 5th (see page 117). The river clubs offer the best in electro, house and rhythm-and-blues. Another waterside district that has become fashionable is the Canal Saint-Martin in the 10th, its quays (Valmy and Jemmapes) and side streets buzzing with interesting restaurants and bars.

Jazz lovers head for the numerous clubs on Rue des Lombards near Les Halles and the famous Caveau de la Huchette (see page 117) on the street of the same name in the Saint-Michel district. Over the decades, jazz legends from all over the world have played here.

⬤ *Rue de la Huchette is full of restaurants, bars, clubs and late-night crowds*

The legendary Moulin Rouge still operates as an entertainment venue

Paris has some 100 dance clubs, so there's something for every music taste, from rock, rap, hip-hop and techno to African rhythms, salsa and samba. Those who like to party all night long should ask bartenders or party-hearty Parisians where the 'after' bars, often unadvertised, are. Many are in the lively Pigalle area of Montmartre.

In a country synonymous with fine wine, wine bars or quiet places to *boire un verre* (have a drink) are plentiful and varied.

The major museums have at least one late-night opening for culture vultures, while the Opéra National de Paris stages the best of opera and ballet performances at its sumptuous Palais Garnier (see pages 72–3) and its modern Opéra Bastille (see page 90), known for its daring productions.

If just vegging out and seeing the latest Hollywood or French film is your thing, Paris has all the major films in *version originale* (VO) in cinemas at such central locations as the 6th *arrondissement*, the Champs-Élysées, Les Halles and Montparnasse.

Scantily clad cancan girls in cabaret-type performances strut their stuff in **Le Lido** (🄰 116 bis av. des Champs-Élysées, 8th 🄣 01 40 76 56 10 🄦 www.lido.fr), **Le Moulin Rouge** (🄰 82 blvd de Clichy, 18th 🄣 01 53 09 82 82 🄦 www.moulinrouge.fr) and **Le Crazy Horse** (🄰 12 av. George V, 8th 🄣 01 47 23 32 32 🄦 www.lecrazyhorseparis.com), among others.

The weekly *Pariscope* or *l'Officiel des Spectacles*, available at newsstands, list the full spectrum of more serious eroticism. These two publications also provide up-to-date listings (only in French) of films, live theatre, exhibitions, sporting events, guided tours and even restaurants.

The main area for gay nightlife is the Marais, though the traditional clubbing focal point is the **Queen** nightclub on the Champs-Élysées (🄰 102 av. des Champs-Élysées, 8th 🄣 01 53 89 08 90 🄦 http://queen.fr).

Sport & relaxation

SPECTATOR SPORTS
Football & rugby

Fans can see professional football and rugby matches at either the Stade de France or the smaller Parc des Princes, the home stadium of the local football team, Paris Saint-Germain.

Parc des Princes ⓐ 24 rue du Commandant Guilbaud, 16th ⓘ 32 75 (within France) ⓦ www.leparcdesprinces.fr ⓝ Metro: Porte de Saint-Cloud

Stade de France ⓐ rue Francis de Pressensé ⓘ 08 92 700 900 ⓦ www.stadefrance.com ⓝ RER: Stade de France

Horse racing

The main courses are the Hippodrome de Longchamp and the Hippodrome d'Auteuil (both in the Bois de Boulogne). For information on all venues, see ⓦ www3.france-galop.com

Hippodrome d'Auteuil ⓐ Butte Mortemart, route d'Auteuil au Lac, 16th ⓘ 01 40 71 47 47 ⓝ Metro: Porte d'Auteuil

Hippodrome de Longchamp ⓐ route des Tribunes, 16th ⓘ 01 44 30 75 00 ⓝ Metro: Porte d'Auteuil

Tennis

The Roland-Garros stadium is the home of the French Open.

Stade Roland-Garros ⓐ 2 av. Gordon-Bennett, 16th ⓘ 08 26 65 00 00 (tickets) ⓦ www.rolandgarros.com ⓝ Metro: Porte d'Auteuil

PARTICIPATION SPORTS
Cycling

Cycling is a popular, convenient recreation, with more than 100 km

(62 miles) of cycle lanes, many bike-rental shops and an excellent Vélib bike loan system (see page 60).

Jogging

Joggers can follow the Seine either down by the riverside or along the streets above. They can also run in and around larger parks such as the Jardin du Luxembourg (see page 100). The Jardin des Tuileries (see pages 64, 67) has a jogging trail.

Rollerblading

More than 4,000 skaters hit the streets every Friday night for an organised skate-athon through the city. Skaters leave from Gare Montparnasse in the 15th *arrondissement* at 22.00 and the full route takes around three hours. See Ⓦ www.pari-roller.com for more information. Beginner skaters should choose the gentler Sunday afternoon events that leave at 14.30 from Place de la Bastille. Skates are available to buy or rent at the Bastille's **Nomades** (ⓐ 37 blvd Bourdon, 4th ⓣ 01 44 54 07 44 Ⓦ www.nomadeshop.com Ⓜ Metro: Bastille).

RELAXATION
Swimming & hammams

You can swim in the River Seine – sort of! The floating **Joséphine Baker** swimming pool (ⓐ Port de la Gare, quai François Mauriac, 13th ⓣ 01 56 61 96 50 Ⓦ www.paris.fr Ⓜ Metro: Quai de la Gare) has a retractable roof for sunny days and is a must-try for keen swimmers.

Alternatively, for a sauna, steam and massage try the Moroccan-style **Les Bains du Marais** (ⓐ 33 rue des Blancs-Manteaux, 4th ⓣ 01 44 61 02 02 Ⓦ www.lesbainsdumarais.fr Ⓛ 10.00–20.00 or 23.00 Ⓜ Metro: Hôtel de Ville or Rambuteau ⓘ Booking essential).

Accommodation

Although international lodging chains are here, most Paris hotels are small, independent establishments. Rooms are often small and lifts can be rickety or non-existent, but generally these hotels have distinct, charming atmospheres. Service can range from surly to warm and accommodating.

Paris also has a great variety of good mid-range, boutique hostelries, with the most attractive called *hôtels de charme*. Many are set in stately old residences, former monasteries, even churches. What these lodgings lack in space, they make up for in character and personal service.

All two-star hotels and above must have staff competent in at least one foreign language, usually English. Reserve as soon as possible, by email or telephone. Internet booking is becoming increasingly popular, with even the small hotels. All hotels post their rates at the entrance and visitors can walk in off the street to book a room, but this is not advisable during holiday seasons.

The Paris Visitors Bureau's excellent website is a good central booking site: ⓦ www.parisinfo.com. Also try ⓦ www.hotels-paris.com

The **Paris Visitors Bureau** (ⓦ www.parisinfo.com) has a central booking site. For small hotels and guesthouses try **Alastair Sawday's Special Places** (ⓦ www.sawdays.co.uk).

PRICE CATEGORIES
Accommodation ratings are based on the average price of a double room per night, including breakfast:
£ up to €100   ££ €100–€200   £££ over €200

A typical hotel façade in Paris with intricate wrought-iron balconies

HOTELS

Hôtel Cluny Sorbonne £ Set in an 18th-century building in the Latin Quarter, the hotel is within walking distance of attractions such as Notre-Dame, the Panthéon and the Louvre. Rimbaud, the great French poet, stayed here in 1872. **ⓐ** 8 rue Victor Cousin, 5th (Left Bank) **ⓣ** 01 43 54 66 66 **ⓦ** www.hotel-cluny.fr **ⓝ** Metro: Cluny La Sorbonne

Hôtel de Nesle £ A hidden gem of a tiny hotel. Each room is individually decorated as if it has been plucked straight from a fairy tale or history book. There's also a hammam. **ⓐ** 7 rue de Nesle, 6th (Left Bank) **ⓣ** 01 43 54 62 41 **ⓦ** www.hoteldenesleparis.com **ⓝ** Metro: Odéon

Hôtel Saint Merry £ This unique hotel in the heart of the historic Marais quarter, originally a presbytery, then a brothel, is in a restored 18th-century stone building with lots of character. **ⓐ** 78 rue de la Verrerie, 4th (Right Bank East) **ⓣ** 01 42 78 14 15 **ⓦ** www.hotel saintmerryparis.com **ⓝ** Metro: Saint-Paul

New Orient Hotel £ This small (30 rooms), charming hotel is in a quiet neighbourhood, but is near a market, restaurants and cafés. Some rooms have balconies. **ⓐ** 16 rue de Constantinople, 8th (Right Bank West) **ⓣ** 01 45 22 21 64 **ⓦ** www.hotel-paris-orient.com **ⓝ** Metro: Europe, Villiers or Saint-Lazare

Caron de Beaumarchais ££ Elaborately decorated, friendly and well located, this hotel is named after the author of *The Marriage of Figaro* (1784), who lived on the same street. **ⓐ** 12 rue Vieille du Temple, 4th (Right Bank East) **ⓣ** 01 42 72 34 12 **ⓦ** www.carondebeaumarchais.com **ⓝ** Metro: Hôtel de Ville or Saint-Paul

⬤ *The charming Caron de Beaumarchais hotel*

Hôtel du 7ème Art ££ This unusual little hotel has a Hollywood theme, with numerous posters, photos and other memorabilia from the golden era of films. ⓐ 20 rue Saint-Paul, 4th (Right Bank East) ⓣ 01 44 54 85 00 ⓦ www.paris-hotel-7art.com ⓝ Metro: Saint-Paul

Hôtel La Sanguine ££ The Sanguine has a convenient location (near Place de la Madeleine) and friendly staff. ⓐ 6 rue de Surène, 8th (Right Bank West) ⓣ 01 42 65 71 61 ⓦ www.hotel-la-sanguine.com ⓝ Metro: Madeleine

Villa Escudier ££ This charming villa, with its studio-type rooms, trees and garden, is far from the city hubbub. ⓐ 64 rue Escudier, Boulogne (Right Bank West) ⓣ 01 48 25 55 33 ⓦ www.villaescudier.com ⓝ Metro: Boulogne-Jean Jaurès

Hôtel Duminy Vendôme ££–£££ Just a few blocks from the Louvre and the Jardin des Tuileries, this comfortable hotel is classic, yet modern, with coffee maker and Wi-Fi in the rooms. ⓐ 3–5 rue du Mont Thabor, 1st (Right Bank West) ⓣ 01 42 60 32 80 ⓦ www.hotelduminy vendome.com ⓝ Metro: Tuileries, Concorde or Madeleine

Hôtel des Marronniers ££–£££ A private courtyard entrance leads to this charming hotel, whose garden is a haven in the centre of the city. ⓐ 21 rue Jacob, 6th (Left Bank) ⓣ 01 43 25 30 60 ⓦ www.hotel-marronniers.com ⓝ Metro: Odéon or Saint-Germain-des-Prés

Hôtel Atala £££ The 48-room Atala near the Champs-Élysées has a bright, cheery garden for fair-weather breakfasting and dining. ⓐ 10 rue de Chateaubriand, 8th (Right Bank West) ⓣ 01 45 62 01 62 ⓦ www.hotel-atala.com ⓝ Metro: Charles de Gaulle-Étoile

Hôtel George V £££ One of the city's premier hotels, for that special occasion. It has a two-Michelin-star restaurant, and exquisite décor throughout. The floral displays are breathtaking. ❸ 31 av. George V, 8th (Right Bank West) ☎ 01 49 52 70 00 🌐 www.fourseasons.com/paris Ⓜ Metro: George V

HOSTELS

A network of youth hostels (*Auberges de Jeunesse*) offers comfortable, inexpensive accommodation for members. There are also numerous youth accommodation centres that don't require membership. The website 🌐 www.parisinfo.com lists hostels, campsites and long-stay apartments. The following are good choices:

3 Ducks Hostel £ Dormitories for four to eight persons, with per-person rates (including breakfast) under €30 per night. ❸ 6 pl. Étienne Pernet, 15th (Left Bank) ☎ 01 48 42 04 05 🌐 www.3ducks.fr Ⓜ Metro: Commerce

Auberge Internationale des Jeunes £ Dorm rooms priced from €14 to €18 per person per night, depending on the time of year. Single rooms are from €38. Breakfast and bedlinen are included. ❸ 10 rue Trousseau, 11th (Right Bank East) ☎ 01 47 00 62 00 🌐 www.aijparis.com Ⓜ Metro: Ledru-Rollin

CAMPSITE
Camping du Bois de Boulogne £ This is the only campsite within Paris. ❸ 2 allée du Bord de l'Eau, 16th (Right Bank West) ☎ 01 45 24 30 00 🌐 www.campingparis.fr Ⓜ Metro: Porte Maillot, then bus 244 or campsite shuttle

THE BEST OF PARIS

TOP 10 ATTRACTIONS

- **Tour Eiffel (Eiffel Tower)** The graceful, filigreed metal tower, glowing burnished gold at night, is the symbol of France around the world (see page 106).

- **Arc de Triomphe** Built to honour Napoleon's victories, this grand, angular arch stands in the centre of 12 avenues, the most famous of which is the Champs-Élysées (see page 62).

- **Notre-Dame** Like a silent sentinel, this magnificent Gothic cathedral on an island in the Seine has witnessed some of France's greatest events (see pages 84–5).

- **Seine** This aquatic artery meandering for 13 km (8 miles) through Paris is the exquisite heart of the city (see page 105).

- **Montmartre** Many visitors may know Montmartre through films, since this, and the adjacent Pigalle, is the famed historic, artistic area of the Moulin Rouge and the picturesque, magical world of Amélie Poulain (see pages 67–8).

- **Musée du Louvre** Once home of the kings of France, the 800-year-old Louvre could be called the king of museums, renowned the world over and housing works from ancient civilisations, the mid-1900s, and everything in between (see pages 70–71).

- **Cimetière du Père-Lachaise** Probably the world's most famous cemetery, Père-Lachaise is the final, beautiful resting place of some of France's most illustrious figures from Balzac to Piaf (see page 83).

- **Quartier Latin (Latin Quarter)** This lively area is the heart of the Left Bank. Once famous for its students and literary legacy, it is now buzzing with cafés and bistros, nightclubs and chic boutiques (see pages 103–5).

- **Musée d'Orsay** The former 19th-century train station is now renowned for its collection of Western art from 1848 to 1914 (see pages 109–11).

- **Markets** Integral to the daily life of Paris are its markets, from abundant fresh food markets to speciality markets selling anything from birds to bric-a-brac (see page 102).

▼ *Notre-Dame cathedral stands right in the centre of Paris*

Suggested itineraries

HALF-DAY: PARIS IN A HURRY

If you have only half a day in Paris, taking the Batobus (see page 105) the length of the Seine from Notre-Dame (see pages 84–5) to the Eiffel Tower (see page 106) or vice versa and visiting each

● *Notre-Dame is beautiful from any angle*

monument at either end will give a compact, visually stunning introduction to Paris.

1 DAY: TIME TO SEE A LITTLE MORE

As well as the Batobus or an hour-long tour on one of the many sightseeing boats, such as the Bâteaux Parisiens (see page 105), you should fit in a half-day tour of either the Musée du Louvre (see pages 70–71) or the Musée d'Orsay (see pages 109–11).

2–3 DAYS: TIME TO SEE MUCH MORE

Adding to one of the above itineraries, climb to the top of the Arc de Triomphe (see page 62) for a real perspective of the grand design of Paris, especially the broad boulevards stretching out like a star. A stroll down the Champs-Élysées, with its elegant shops and cafés, is a must. Over on the Left Bank, do as the Parisians do, visit a gallery or museum, then have a coffee at one of the famous literary cafés (see pages 113–15), watching the *beau monde* go by and soaking up the ambience of the Latin Quarter.

LONGER: ENJOYING PARIS TO THE FULL

Explore the *butte* (or hill) of Paris at Montmartre, where Place du Tertre behind the white-domed Sacré-Coeur is the quintessential Parisian painters' corner. Licensed painters sell portraits or depictions of your favourite Parisian scene. From in front of the Sacré-Coeur, the rooftops of Paris stretch out below. Montmartre, with its climbing cobbled streets, is a great area to have a coffee or a meal.

If you have time to explore beyond Paris, you may wish to visit Versailles, the grand château and gardens built for Louis XIV, particularly if you can time your visit for the Grandes Eaux Musicales (see page 9) or the Nocturnes (see page 10).

Something for nothing

In Paris many wonderful experiences are there for the taking. Thanks to a recent law, national museums and monuments are now free to residents of EU countries aged 18–25 inclusive. For everyone else, they are free on the first Sunday of every month. These include the Louvre, the Musée d'Orsay and the Panthéon among many others. Every Wednesday night the Maison Européenne de la Photographie has free entrance from 17.00 to 20.00.

The permanent collections of all of Paris's municipal museums are also free. One of these, the **Musée Carnavalet** (🅰 23 rue de Sévigné, 3rd ⊕ 01 44 59 58 58 ⊚ www.carnavalet.paris.fr), displays the history of Paris from the French Revolution to today. If you are interested in fashion, the **Palais Galliera** (🅰 10 av. Pierre 1er de Serbie, 16th ⊕ 01 56 52 86 20 ⊚ www.galliera.paris.fr) displays three centuries of history gratis, but check before you go as the fragility of the costumes does not allow the museum to be opened to the public year-round.

In the Marais district is the 17th-century Place des Vosges. Ruddy-pink brick pavilions form a handsome square that is both a peaceful public space and a collection of art galleries. Nobility and literary figures, such as Victor Hugo, lived here and his house is now a museum.

Nearby, the fence along the famous Jardin du Luxembourg has become an outdoor photo gallery. Huge photographs, many by news photographers and photojournalists, are exhibited. Each is lit at night, providing an enchanting nocturnal experience.

During Paris's long, sultry summers, free concerts are held in some 20 parks and gardens and there is often a Latin or African drumbeat to be heard along the quays of central Paris.

The city itself is a walkable feast, and perhaps nowhere can you get more value for your nothing spent than strolling along the Seine. Each side of the river, from the Notre-Dame curving westward to the Eiffel Tower, provides a panorama of some of the world's most famous buildings and of the bridges that link Left Bank to Right.

▲ *Under the Louvre's Pyramid – free entry on the first Sunday of each month*

When it rains

Rainy days are no problem in Paris, filled as it is with so many wonderful museums. Most are open through the weekend (closing on either Monday or Tuesday), and many, such as the Louvre, the Musée d'Orsay and the Maillol, have charming cafés to lounge in.

A particularly atmospheric retreat is the fifth-floor Rivoli restaurant in the BHV department store near the Hôtel de Ville. The Rivoli's star attraction is the panoramic view of the Paris rooftops, particularly the Hôtel de Ville, the Panthéon and many old buildings with their mansard roofs and chimneypots. Parisian cafés and brasseries in general are an integral part of the soul of the city. Simple, traditional establishments or fancier venues with polished brass and wood fittings are wonderful places to escape the rain, relax and watch life go by.

One way to get an instant briefing on Paris on a rainy day is to catch a screening of the excellent film **Paris Story** (❸ 11 bis rue Scribe, 9th ❶ 01 42 66 62 06 Ⓦ www.paris-story.com ❶ Hourly 10.00–18.00 Ⓝ Metro: Opéra). In this multimedia promenade through Paris's past, 2,000 years of history plays out on a giant screen, with the character of Victor Hugo narrating.

Even for non-shoppers, the glass-covered passages of Paris are a delightful legacy of the early 19th century. Originally constructed to protect shoppers from wet weather, they still do so today, while housing luxury goods and boutiques. Among the most charming of the remaining arcades are the boutique-filled **Grand-Cerf** (❸ 145 rue Saint-Denis, 2nd Ⓦ www.passagedugrandcerf.com ❶ 08.30–20.00 Mon–Sat) and the *galeries* **Colbert** and **Vivienne** (❸ 6 & 4 rue des Petits-Champs, 2nd Ⓦ http://galerie-vivienne.com ❶ Mon–Sat), known for book collections and haute couture.

⬢ *Try the Rivoli restaurant in the BHV department store*

On arrival

TIME DIFFERENCE

Paris is on European standard time (GMT plus one hour). Daylight saving applies, with clocks going forward one hour in spring and back one hour in autumn, on the same date as the UK.

ARRIVING

By air

Paris has two main airports, **Roissy-Charles de Gaulle** (CDG) north of the city, and **Orly** (ORY) to the south (ℹ 39 50 within France; 01 70 36 39 50 from abroad Ⓦ www.adp.fr). The easiest way to the city centre from both is by RER (commuter train) line B. The line goes to Gare du Nord, Châtelet (Right Bank), Saint-Michel and Luxembourg (Left Bank). There are metro connections from these stations.

Those not travelling light can take **Air France buses** (Ⓦ www.cars-airfrance.com), which leave from CDG every 15 minutes for Porte Maillot and Charles de Gaulle-Étoile (Arc de Triomphe), or for the train stations of Gare de Lyon and Gare Montparnasse. There is also a service from Orly to Montparnasse, Invalides and Charles de

⬤ *The River Seine cuts through Paris*

Gaulle-Étoile. **RATP** (Ⓦ www.ratp.fr) also operates cheap bus services: the Roissybus from CDG to Rue Scribe (behind Opéra) and the Orlybus from Orly to Denfert-Rochereau.

The most comfortable way to get to the city is by taxi. From the CDG airport to the centre of Paris will cost about €25 to €45 depending on traffic conditions. There is a surcharge after 19.00 on Sundays and public holidays. Many drivers don't speak much English, so have your destination address written out. Taxis from Orly will be about €20 to €30 with normal traffic conditions. Drivers usually charge a fee for bags. Avoid touts inside the airport offering taxi or limousine service, as you will invariably end up paying much more. Go to the taxi ranks outside the terminal instead.

Several companies provide a minivan service, with delivery to hotels, but you have to book in advance, and you may have to share with other passengers (see Ⓦ www.parishuttle.com).

Some charter airlines, and Ryanair, use **Beauvais airport** (ⓘ 08 92 68 20 66 Ⓦ www.aeroportbeauvais.com), which is quite far from the city. Buses leave from the airport car park for the city shortly after each landing. You can also use a combination of taxi and train to get to Gare du Nord. For return flights, buses leave from the Pershing car park near the Palais des Congrès. You need to get there around

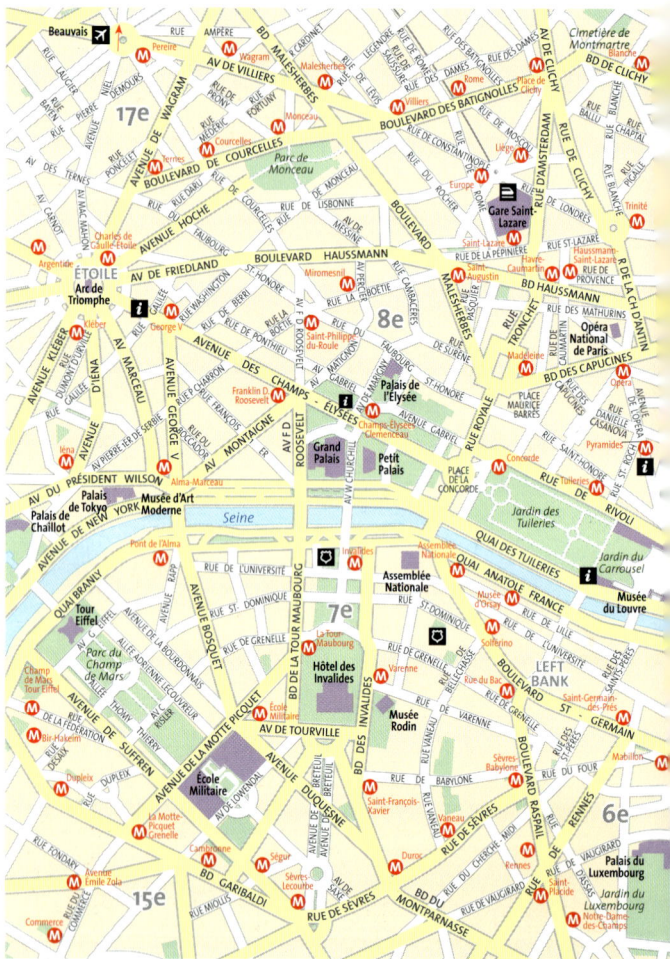

Beauvais

RUE AMPÈRE
BD CARNOT
RUE CABANEL

RUE CAULINCOURT
RUE PIERRE DEMOURS

Wagram
AV DE VILLIERS
Malesherbes
Place de Clichy
BD DE CLICHY

Cimetière de Montmartre
Blanche

17e
Monceau
BOULEVARD DES BATIGNOLLES
Villiers
Rome
Liège

AV DES TERNES
BOULEVARD DE COURCELLES
Courcelles
Parc de Monceau

AVENUE HOCHE
BOULEVARD HAUSSMANN
Gare Saint-Lazare

Charles de Gaulle-Étoile
Argentine
ÉTOILE
Arc de Triomphe
AV DE FRIEDLAND
Miromesnil
Saint-Lazare
RUE DE LA PÉPINIÈRE
Havre-Caumartin
Haussmann-Saint-Lazare
RUE DE PROVENCE
BD HAUSSMANN

Kléber
George V
8e
Saint-Philippe-du-Roule
Saint-Augustin
Madeleine
Opéra National de Paris
RUE DES MATHURINS
BD DES CAPUCINES
Opéra

AVENUE KLÉBER
AVENUE D'IÉNA
AVENUE MARCEAU
AVENUE DES CHAMPS
Franklin D. Roosevelt
ÉLYSÉES
Palais de l'Élysée
PLACE MAURICE BARRÈS
Pyramides

Iéna
AVENUE GEORGE V
AV MONTAIGNE
Alma-Marceau
Grand Palais
Champs-Élysées-Clemenceau
Concorde
RUE ST-HONORÉ

AV DU PRÉSIDENT WILSON
Palais de Tokyo
Musée d'Art Moderne
Petit Palais
PLACE DE LA CONCORDE
RUE DE RIVOLI

AVENUE DE NEW YORK
Palais de Chaillot
Seine
Jardin des Tuileries
Jardin du Carrousel

Pont de l'Alma
QUAI DES TUILERIES
Musée du Louvre

QUAI BRANLY
RUE DE L'UNIVERSITÉ
Invalides
Assemblée Nationale
QUAI ANATOLE FRANCE
Musée d'Orsay

Tour Eiffel
AVENUE DE LA BOURDONNAIS
RUE ST-DOMINIQUE
7e
La Tour Maubourg
RUE DE LILLE
Solférino
LEFT BANK

Parc du Champ de Mars
RUE DE GRENELLE
Hôtel des Invalides
Varenne
Rue du Bac
Saint-Germain-des-Prés
GERMAIN

Champ de Mars Tour Eiffel
AVENUE DE LA FÉDÉRATION
Bir-Hakeim
BD DES INVALIDES
Musée Rodin
RUE DE VARENNE
BOULEVARD RASPAIL
Mabillon

Dupleix
AVENUE DE SUFFREN
Sèvres Babylone
BOULEVARD DU FOUR
6e

La Motte Picquet Grenelle
École Militaire
AV DE TOURVILLE
Saint-François-Xavier
RUE DE SÈVRES
RENNES

RUE FONDARY
Avenue Émile Zola
BD GARIBALDI
Ségur
Duroc
Palais du Luxembourg

Commerce
15e
Sèvres Lecourbe
Falguière
RUE DE SÈVRES
BD DU MONTPARNASSE
Jardin du Luxembourg
Notre-Dame-des-Champs

Paris

0   500 metres
0   500 yards

MONTMARTRE

RUE DE LA GOUTTE D'OR

BOULEVARD DE LA CHAPELLE

La Chapelle

Charles de Gaulle

Louis Blanc

Abbesses

Anvers

BD DE ROCHECHOUART

Pigalle

Barbès Rochechouart

AV TRUDAINE

9e

Gare du Nord

10e

Gare du Nord

Gare de l'Est

RUE LA FAYETTE

Château-Landon

Gare de l'Est

Jaurès

Bolivar

Buttes Chaumont

AVENUE SIMON BOLIVAR

Colonel Fabien

BD DE LA VILLETTE

Saint-Georges

Poissonnière

Notre-Dame-de-Lorette

RUE LA FAYETTE

Cadet

RUE DE PARADIS

2e

Le Peletier

Richelieu-Drouot

RUE RICHER

RUE DES PETITES ÉCURIES

BD MONTMARTRE

RUE BERGÈRE

RUE D'ENGHIEN

BD DE STRASBOURG

BD DE MAGENTA

RÉBEVAL

Belleville

BD DE BELLEVILLE

Quatre-Septembre

Grands Boulevards

Bonne Nouvelle

BD DE BONNE NOUVELLE

Bourse

Bourse des Valeurs

Réaumur Sébastopol

Strasbourg Saint-Denis

ST-MARTIN

Jacques Bonsergent

RÉPUBLIQUE

RUE DU FAUBOURG DU TEMPLE

Couronnes

Palais Royal

LES HALLES

1er

Sentier

Arts et Métiers

Temple

3e

AVENUE DE LA RÉPUBLIQUE

Parmentier

Oberkampf

Étienne Marcel

RUE DE TURBIGO

Palais Royal Les Halles

Les Halles

Rambuteau

Saint-Maur

Centre Pompidou

RIGHT BANK

Archives Nationales

BOULEVARD VOLTAIRE

Saint-Ambroise

RUE DE RIVOLI

Hôtel de Ville

L'HÔTEL DE VILLE

Musée Carnavalet

Saint-Sébastien-Froissart

11e

Voltaire

CITÉ

Palais de Justice

Notre-Dame

Saint-Paul

RUE SAINT-ANTOINE

BD BEAUMARCHAIS

4e

Bastille

BASTILLE

QUAI DES CÉLESTINS

RUE DE LYON

Odéon

St-Michel Notre-Dame

Cluny La Sorbonne

BOULEVARD ST-GERMAIN

Maubert Mutualité

Institut du Monde Arabe

AVENUE DAUMESNIL

Sorbonne

QUARTIER LATIN

Orly

Panthéon

5e

Universités

Seine

Quai de la Rapée

Legend

- ......POI
- M .....Metro Stop
- .....Cathedral
- i .....Information
- .....Police Station
- .....Airport
- .....Railway Stn
- .....Hospital

three and a quarter hours before your flight departure time in order to be at the airport one and a half or two hours in advance.

By rail

Those travelling to Paris on the Eurostar arrive at Gare du Nord, which has metro, RER and bus connections to pretty much anywhere in the city. Alternatively, turn right off the platform to find the taxi rank. Be prepared to queue.

By road

Driving into, or around, Paris is not for the faint-hearted. Traffic is heavy and hectic, parking spaces are hard to find and the one-way systems can be complex. If you still wish to drive, the main roads into Paris all reach the *périphérique* (ring road), which has various exits to different parts of the city. Those arriving from the UK by car will probably use the A1 from the north.

Despite competition from the Chunnel, ferry and hydrofoil services continue to take cars and foot passengers across the English Channel.

FINDING YOUR FEET

There are tourist office welcome centres at Gare du Nord, Gare de l'Est, Gare de Lyon, Pyramides, Anvers and Porte de Versailles, all of which provide free maps. There are also summer kiosks at Trocadéro, Notre-Dame, Hôtel de Ville and Bastille. The telephone answering service is available 24 hours a day on ☎ 08 92 68 30 00. Another useful information helpline is ☎ 39 75 (dialled only from within France).

Violent crime is generally rare, but areas around train and bus stations, particularly Gare du Nord, have an increasing reputation for violence at night. There are many pickpockets in Paris, especially

IF YOU GET LOST, TRY …

Excuse me, do you speak English?
Excusez-moi, vous parlez anglais?
Ekskewzehmwah, voopahrlay ohnglay?

Excuse me, is this the right way to the city centre/the tourist office/the station/the bus station?
Excusez-moi, c'est la bonne direction pour le centre-ville/
l'office de tourisme/la gare/la gare routière?
*Ekskewzehmwah, seh lah bon deerekseeawng poor ler sahngtr
veel/lohfeece de tooreezm/lah gahr/lah gahr rootyair?*

Can you point to it on my map?
Pouvez-vous me le montrer sur la carte?
Poovehvoo mer ler mawngtreh sewr lah kart?

on the metro during rush hours and at crowded tourist attractions. Leave valuables in the hotel or room safe. Always be vigilant and keep bags and wallets closed and out of reach. Don't be obvious: carrying big bulky cameras and purses will attract pickpockets.

Always go to an official sales point to buy tickets, and avoid touts. If you encounter any problems, look for a uniformed police officer, transport security staff or ticket sales staff.

ORIENTATION

Paris is divided into 20 *arrondissements* (districts). The 1st is the centre of the city, and the others are laid out in a clockwise spiral from

B3: Aéroport Charles de Gaulle 2
B5: Mitry-Claye

RER

La Courneuve-
8 Mai 1945 — 7

Bobigny-Pablo
Picasso — 5

A Communicarta
Style45 design

12 Porte de la
Chapelle

Marx
Dormoy

Corentin Cariou

Hoche

E2: Chelles-Gournay
E4: Tournan

RER

Porte de Pantin

7b

Pré-Saint-Gervais

Mairie des Lilas

Crimée

Ourcq

Danube

11

Laumière

Bolivar

Buttes
Chaumont

Place des Fêtes

La Chapelle

Riquet

Stalingrad

Jaurès

Louis Blanc 7b

Magenta

Château-Landon

Gare de l'Est (Verdun)

Château d'Eau

Strasbourg Saint-Denis

Réaumur
Sébastopol

Étienne Marcel

Rambuteau

Les Halles

Châtelet 11

Pont
Neuf

Cité

St-Michel-Notre-Dame

Châtelet
(Pont au Change)

Hôtel de Ville

Maubert-Mutualité

Odéon

Saint-
Germain-
des-Prés

Saint
Sulpice

Saint
Placide

Vavin

Raspail

Edgar
Quinet

Goncourt
(Hôpital Saint-Louis)

Jacques
Bonsergent

République

Arts et
Métiers

Temple

Filles du
Calvaire

Saint-Sébastien-
Froissart

Chemin Vert

Saint-Paul
(Le Marais)

Bastille

Oberkampf

Rue
Saint-Maur

St Ambroise

Voltaire (Léon Blum)

Charonne

Rue des Boulets

Richard
Lenoir

Bréguet-Sabin

Ledru
Rollin

Faidherbe-
Chaligny

Reuilly-
Diderot

Botzaris

Jourdain

Colonel Fabien

Belleville

Pyrénées

Couronnes

Ménilmontant

Père Lachaise

Philippe Auguste

Alexandre
Dumas

Avron

Nation
(Place des Antilles)

Parmentier

Gallieni
(Parc de Bagnolet) 3

9 Mairie de Montreuil

1 Château de
Vincennes

A2: Boissy-Saint-Léger
A4: Marne-la-Vallée/Chessy
(Parc Disneyland®)

RER

Nation 2 6

Picpus
(Courteline)

Bel-Air

Gare de Lyon

Quai de
la Rapée

Montgallet

Daumesnil
(Félix Éboué)

Michel Bizot

Porte Dorée

Créteil
(Pointe du Lac) 8

Cité

Pont
Marie

Sully-
Morland

Gare
d'Austerlitz 10

Dugommier

Bercy

Cour Saint-
Émilion

Quai de
la Gare

Bibliothèque François
Mitterrand

D2: Melun
D4: Malesherbes
D6: Corbeil Essonnes

RER

Cluny-
La Sorbonne

Cardinal
Lemoine

Jussieu

Luxembourg
(Sénat)

Place Monge

Censier-Daubenton

Port-Royal

Saint-
Marcel

Campo-
Formio

Chevaleret

Nationale

Les Gobelins

Denfert-
Rochereau

Glacière

Corvisart

14

Olympiades

Saint-Jacques

Mouton-
Duvernet

Alésia

Cité
Universitaire

RER

Tolbiac

Maison Blanche

Porte d'Italie

C2: Massy Palaiseau
C4: Dourdan-la-Forêt
C6: St-Martin d'Étampes
C8: Versailles Chantier

RER

B2: Robinson
B4: Saint-Rémy-lès-Chevreuse

5 Place d'Italie

4 Porte d'Orléans

7 Villejuif Louis Aragon

Mairie d'Ivry 7

there. As the *arrondissements* are so basic to the layout of Paris, they are constantly referred to in guides and literature, almost always using simply their associated number (1st, 2nd, etc, as in the addresses in this guide). The Seine divides the city into Left and Right Banks.

The best way to get to know Paris is to walk around your hotel neighbourhood. Paris is like a series of villages, each with its own attraction and character. Then you can begin to explore further afield by public transport. The main city thoroughfares include the Champs-Élysées and Boulevard Haussmann on the Right Bank, and boulevards Saint-Germain and Saint-Michel on the Left.

Paris is a small city, easy to navigate on foot. You can walk across it from east to west or north to south in one day, if you don't stop for sightseeing. However, it is not always pedestrian-friendly, so it is important to be alert, especially at crossings.

If you get lost, some metro stops have maps displaying the immediate area. You can also get your bearings from the Eiffel Tower, Arc de Triomphe, Panthéon, Notre-Dame or Tour Montparnasse.

GETTING AROUND

Paris has an excellent metro system reaching all parts of the city. The 14 lines are identified by number and colour. The RER commuter trains connect to the suburbs. An RATP 'Paris Visite' is a travel pass for one, two, three or five consecutive days on metro, bus and RER trains. If you buy a Paris Visite pass for zones 1–6, it also includes trips to the airport. For zones 1–3 only, a one-day adult pass is currently €9.30 and a five-day pass €29.90. For zones 1–6, a one-day pass is €19.60 and a five-day pass €51.20. Paris Visite also includes discounts on tickets for the Arc de Triomphe, a Seine cruise and purchases at Galeries Lafayette.

Alternatively, you can buy single tickets (€1.70) which can be used for one journey by metro, RER or bus in zones one and two, including connections (except those between metro and bus). A *carnet* (book) of ten tickets is better value at €12.50. Keep your ticket until you have completed your journey; on the RER and some metro stations you will need it to exit the system. Note that the entire Paris metro network is a no-smoking zone.

Route maps for buses are available free in metro stations, and you can hail taxis in the street or at taxi ranks. One of the best ways of getting around Paris, however, is the 'hop-on, hop-off' bike loan

● *Even the underground stations are pretty*

PARIS IN THE MOVIES

If, on a first trip to Paris, you find that various parts of the city are weirdly familiar, it doesn't necessarily mean that the reincarnationists are right: the city has formed the backdrop to so many popular films over the years that you could easily have absorbed its picturesque settings simply by spending rainy afternoons curled up in front of the TV.

Paris is all over films, and this is apt when you consider that commercial cinema was born here, when Louis and Auguste Lumière projected their first films in the basement of the Grand Café on the Boulevard des Capucines in 1895. Since then, more than 400 major motion pictures have been shot among Paris's tree-lined boulevards and broad quays.

Many have depicted the clichéd Paris of accordion music, the cancan and the wise-cracking prostitute with a heart of gold; and the city lends itself to the visual commonplace too. Countless films use establishing shots of Gustave Eiffel's imposing wrought-iron tower, and another popular backdrop, the Seine, is also overfamiliar to film fans.

Robert Altman's 1994 *Prêt-à-Porter* may have been a box-office flop, but at least it managed to juxtapose unglamorous images of the city's traffic jams, rain and grey skies with an idyllic, tourist-video vision of its scenery. As the city changes, films become unwitting historical documents: take, for example, the 1963 comedy *Irma la Douce* (featuring the saintly hooker figure); this has preserved excellent images of the giant food markets of Les Halles, which moved out of central Paris in 1969.

Paris is fabulous if you want to explore themes that are in any way to do with sex. Its seamier aspects are perfect for portraying windswept-and-interesting desires, hence Brando's pursuit of Maria Schneider along the Bir-Hakeim Bridge in Bernardo Bertolucci's darkly erotic *Last Tango in Paris* (1972). In fact, Paris's sometimes-brooding majesty often manages to disguise the essential ludicrousness of such films.

Numerous films are set in the clubs of racy, *fin-de-siècle* Paris and gain atmosphere from the city's reputation for sauciness. The 1952 *Moulin Rouge*, with José Ferrer as diminutive poster boy Toulouse-Lautrec, evokes Paris's raunchy belle époque nightlife so vividly that it's planted images of absinthe, smoky cabarets, raffish sociopaths and slinky *chanteuses* in many impressionable minds. As unrealistic as it was, it conveyed more truth than the computer-generated, too-comfortable Paris of 2001's *Moulin Rouge*.

Amélie, the big French hit of 2001, takes place in a *moulin* of a different sort, just a few minutes' walk from the infamous club. The film's elfin heroine devises her altruistic schemes at the Café Tabac des Deux Moulins on 15 rue Lepic, which is now on many a cinephile's must-see list. The bar and the rest of this lively *quartier* are clearly recognisable all through the film. One awaits a sequel, in which impish Amélie's purity of soul will have led her to the inevitable career change, as we see her walking Paris's cinematic streets in fishnets and a red beret, transforming the lives of her diminutive-but-raffish punters by curing their addiction to absinthe with a blast on her accordion. Cliché, of course, but the urban scenery will be fantastic.

system called **Vélib** (☏ 01 30 79 79 30 Ⓦ www.velib.paris.fr). There are bike stations spread around the city where you may collect or deposit a bike, as well as a good network of cycle paths. Follow the instructions on the machine (you will need a credit card). Bicycles are charged by the hour at fairly low rates. And it's great fun!

SNCF trains to out-of-town areas depart from the following *gares* (stations): Gare du Nord, Gare de l'Est, Saint-Lazare, Lyon, Austerlitz and Montparnasse.

RATP Information on buses, metro and RER commuter trains in Paris ☏ 32 46 within France; 08 92 69 32 46 from abroad Ⓦ www.ratp.fr

SNCF Information on trains in Île-de-France and nationwide ☏ 36 35 within France; 08 91 36 20 20 from abroad Ⓦ www.transilien.com (Île-de-France) or www.voyages-sncf.com (nationwide)

Car hire

It is not a good idea to rent a car to use in Paris or to get to out-of-town places. For travelling around Île-de-France or throughout the country, it is better to take the excellent, efficient SNCF trains and hire a car at your destination.

If you do wish to hire a car in Paris, you will find all the major car-rental companies here, all with offices at Charles de Gaulle airport. Rates range from about €30 a day up to more than €100.

Ada ☏ 01 43 47 58 80 (Gare de Lyon) Ⓦ www.ada.fr

Avis ☏ 01 42 77 06 06 Ⓦ www.avis.com

Europcar ☏ 01 49 65 63 23 Ⓦ www.europcar.com

Hertz ☏ 01 47 03 49 12 Ⓦ www.hertz.com

National/Citer ☏ 01 53 20 06 52 (Gare du Nord); 01 48 62 65 81 (Roissy-Charles de Gaulle airport) Ⓦ www.nationalcar.com

---

◐ *The Panthéon dominates the Paris skyline*

THE CITY OF
Paris

Right Bank West

The traditional separation of Paris into Left and Right Bank, between business and culture, is no longer valid. The Left Bank still has more of the universities (especially the Sorbonne) and the bohemian cafés, but today the Right Bank also has artistic areas, especially the Marais and the Bastille. Both sides of the Seine have their distinct charm and attractions. For ease of sightseeing, we have divided the city into three areas: Right Bank West, Right Bank East and Left Bank.

Under the direction of Napoleon III, Baron Georges Haussmann reshaped and modernised Paris. His work is most obvious in this area of the city, with its broad, tree-lined boulevards, magnificent monuments, grand mansions and open gardens. Some of the city's greatest sights are found here, such as the Louvre, the Champs-Élysées and Arc de Triomphe, Montmartre and the Sacré-Coeur.

SIGHTS & ATTRACTIONS

Arc de Triomphe

Built to honour Napoleon's victories, this grand arch is the centrepiece of 12 boulevards that radiate 360 degrees from it. It also lies in a perfectly straight line along an axis from the Arc de Triomphe du Carrousel, near the Louvre, out to the Grande Arche de la Défense, to the west. Stairs lead 50 m (164 ft) up to its roof for a panoramic view of the symmetry of Paris. La Voie Royale runs from the Louvre to the modern Grande Arche in Place de la Défense. Beneath the Arc de Triomphe, a flame burns for an unknown soldier from World War I. As with most national museums in Paris, admission is free for residents of EU countries aged 18–25.

ⓐ pl. Charles de Gaulle, 8th ❶ 01 55 37 73 77 Ⓦ www.monum.fr

Right Bank West

0   500 metres
0   500 yards

10e

POI
Metro Stop
Information
Police Station
Railway Stn
Bus Station
Hospital

Gare du Nord

Marché aux Puces de la Porte de Clignancourt

Funiculaire
Musée du Vieux Montmartre (12 rue Cortot) & Sacré-Cœur
Place des Abbesses

BD DE MAGENTA

BD DE CLICHY

9e

Folies Bergères

Mairie du 9e

2e

Bourse

Banque de France

Mairie du 2e

Musée des Arts et Métiers

Musée de la Poupée

Centre Pompidou

Hôtel de Ville

Église Saint-Eustache

Forum des Halles

Mairie du 1er

Sainte-Chapelle

Conciergerie

1er

Galeries Lafayette

Opéra

Palais Royal

Pyramide Musée du Louvre

Musée du Louvre

Place Vendôme

La Colonne

Gare Saint-Lazare

Mairie du 8e Saint-Augustin

Ministère de l'Intérieur

Place de la Madeleine

Galerie Nationale du Jeu de Paume

Jardin des Tuileries

Musée de l'Orangerie

7e

Musée d'Orsay

Mairie du 7e

Assemblée Nationale

PONT DE LA CONCORDE

BOULEVARD SAINT-GERMAIN

QUAI ANATOLE FRANCE

Palais de la Découverte

Grand Palais

Petit Palais

PONT ALEXANDRE III

Esplanade des Invalides

Hôtel des Invalides

8e

Musée Nissim de Camondo

Musée Jacquemart-André

Parc Monceau

Université Paris IV Sorbonne

AV FRANKLIN D ROOSEVELT

BD DE LA TOUR MAUBOURG

Université Paris IV Sorbonne

17e

Arc de Triomphe

Palais Galliera

Musée d'Art Moderne

Palais de Tokyo

PONT DE L'ALMA

AVENUE GEORGE V

AV MARCEAU

AVENUE D'IÉNA

Panthéon Bouddhique

Musée National des Arts Asiatiques Guimet

Musée Dapper

Musée Marmottan Monet

Palais de Chaillot

Jardins du Trocadéro

Tour Eiffel

Parc du Champ de Mars

Champ de Mars

Palais des Congrès de Paris

AVENUE MAC MAHON

AVENUE FOCH

La Seine

N

🕐 10.00–23.00 summer; 10.00–22.30 winter Ⓜ Metro: Charles de Gaulle-Étoile

Champs-Élysées

This is the grandest of the boulevards that stretch away from the Arc de Triomphe. Luxury boutiques and car showrooms, nightclubs and the *beau monde* are all here. Having a coffee on 'the Champs' isn't cheap, but the passing parade is worth the price. At night, with the Arc floodlit in golden light, the Champs is certainly impressive. However, despite the boulevard's grand demeanour, not all prices are grand. You can have a lot of good, clean fun on the Champs. Ⓜ Metro: Charles de Gaulle-Étoile

Conciergerie

One of the oldest buildings in Paris, the conical-towered Conciergerie on the Île de la Cité, once a palace, became a prison during the French Revolution. Among the 2,800 prisoners held here, the most famous was Marie-Antoinette, who was taken to the guillotine at Place de la Concorde. Her cell can be seen today. Guided visits in English are available by prior reservation. 🅐 2 blvd du Palais, 1st ☎ 01 53 40 60 80 🌐 www.monum.fr 🕐 09.30–18.00 Ⓜ Metro: Cité

Jardin des Tuileries

The Tuileries, Paris's oldest park, forms an orderly sweep of greenery, gardens and statues leading up to the Louvre, affording wonderful views of the museum buildings in one direction and the Arc de Triomphe in the other. The park is also a sculpture garden, with works by Rodin, Henry Moore and Max Ernst, among others. The most recent addition is Giuseppe Penone's *Arbre des Voyelles* (*The Vowel Tree*), a bronze fallen tree. At its western end, the park

⬤ *Old and new sculptural forms to enjoy in the Jardin des Tuileries*

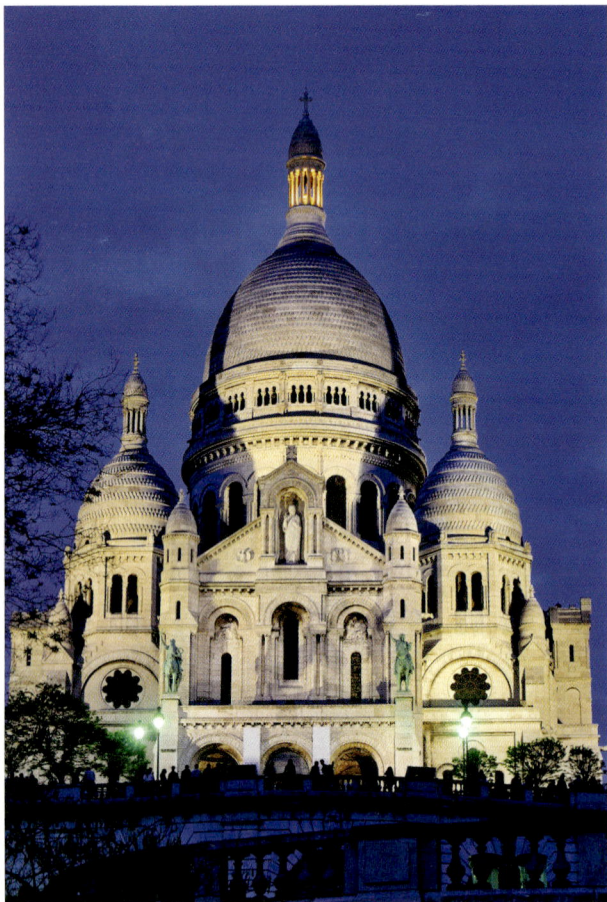

The cupolas of the majestic Sacré-Coeur are floodlit at night

is graced by the exhibition spaces **Galerie Nationale du Jeu de Paume** (Ⓦ www.jeudepaume.org), displaying photography and contemporary art exhibitions, and the **Musée de l'Orangerie** (Ⓦ www.musee-orangerie.fr), with paintings by Monet, Renoir and Picasso among others. ❷ rue de Rivoli, 1st ⓛ Gardens: 07.30–21.00 (summer) (until 23.45 Mon–Fri, until 00.45 Sat & Sun July & Aug); 07.30–19.30 (winter) Ⓜ Metro: Tuileries or Concorde

Montmartre

This historic district in the 18th *arrondissement*, called the 'balcony of Paris', is characterised by the Sacré-Coeur, steep streets lined with ancient buildings, and a lively buzz from the tourists and locals congregating at terrace cafés, restaurants, crowded boutiques and around the basilica. This is the area immortalised by Toulouse-Lautrec in his paintings and posters of the Moulin Rouge (still extant and still saucy) and thrilling cancan girls. Nearby Pigalle advertises in loud neon its sex shows and wares. Like a cartoon locomotive, the little white Montmartrain tootles through the cobbled streets, giving commentary in several languages. It departs in front of the Sacré-Coeur or Place Pigalle (☎ 01 48 00 90 80).

Crowning Montmartre with white cupolas, the basilica of **Sacré-Coeur** (❷ 35 rue du Chevalier-de-la-Barre, 18th ☎ 01 53 41 89 00 Ⓦ www.sacre-coeur-montmartre.com ⓛ Basilica: 06.00–22.30; dome: 09.30–20.15 Thur–Mon, 09.30–18.30 Tues & Wed; crypt: 11.00–20.00 Thur–Mon, 12.00–18.30 Tues & Wed Ⓜ Metro: Anvers or Abbesses) is one of the most visible of Paris's landmarks. It is especially beautiful on bright, blue days or glowing pearl-white at night. Those with the energy can climb up the main rotunda. At weekends, especially in summer, the grounds of the basilica are crowded with sightseers, entertained by performers and buskers.

Place du Tertre is an ancient square just west of the Sacré-Coeur and is the quintessential artist-with-easel scene. Its picture-postcard ambience has made it crowded, though, so you may have to take a rest in one of the neighbourhood cafés or wine bars. There is even a tiny vineyard between Rue des Saules and Rue Saint-Vincent.

If you're hanging out for some retail therapy, boutiques in Place des Abbesses, west of the Sacré-Coeur, have a relaxed atmosphere on Sundays, when most Paris shops are closed.

Place de la Concorde

The golden-tipped obelisk in the centre is actually a 3,200-year-old Egyptian relic from Luxor. This bright, grand square has a bloody history: during the French Revolution, more than 1,000 people were guillotined here, including King Louis XVI and Marie-Antoinette. Ⓜ Metro: Concorde

Sainte-Chapelle

This delicate gem among Paris churches is renowned for its 13th-century stained-glass windows, whose 15-m (49-ft) compositions fill the chapel with jewels of light. ⓐ 6 blvd du Palais, 1st ⓣ 01 53 40 60 80 ⓦ www.monum.fr ⓛ 09.30–18.00 (summer); 09.00–17.00 (winter) Ⓜ Metro: Cité

Tenniseum

The Stade Roland-Garros, where the French Open is held, is open for visits when there are no matches. The first multimedia tennis museum, the Tenniseum, covers some 2,200 sq m (23,681 sq ft). There are also guided tours of the museum and stadium, including backstage (book in advance). ⓐ 2 av. Gordon-Bennett, 16th ⓣ 01 47 43 48 48 ⓦ www.fft.fr or www.rolandgarros.com ⓛ 10.00–18.00 Wed & Fri–Sun; school holidays: 10.00–18.00 Tues–Sun Ⓜ Metro: Porte d'Auteuil

Trocadéro

A half-moon-shaped structure on the Right Bank facing the Eiffel Tower, the Palais de Chaillot (better known as the Trocadéro) was built for the 1937 Exposition Universelle. It houses the **Musée de l'Homme** (① 01 44 05 72 72 ⓦ www.museedelhomme.fr ⓘ Due to reopen after renovations in 2014), **Musée National de la Marine** (① 01 53 65 69 69 ⓦ www.musee-marine.fr ② 11.00–18.00 Mon & Wed–Thur, 11.00–21.30 Fri, 11.00–19.00 Sat & Sun), **Théâtre National de Chaillot** (① 01 53 65 30 00 ⓦ http://theatre-chaillot.fr) and **Cité de l'Architecture et du Patrimoine** (① 01 58 51 52 00 ⓦ www.citechaillot.fr ② 11.00–19.00 Fri–Mon & Wed, 11.00–21.00 Thur). In summer, people chill out around the Trocadéro's cool pools and lawns. The central square, where the wings of the building cleave in two, reveals a magnificent view of the Eiffel Tower. ② 1 pl. du Trocadéro, 16th ⓜ Metro: Trocadéro

CULTURE

Galeries Nationales du Grand Palais

With its splendid belle époque glass roof visible along the Seine's Right Bank, this grand palace built for the 1900 World Fair holds major art exhibitions. ② 3 av. du Général Eisenhower, 8th ① 01 44 13 17 17 ⓦ www.rmn.fr ② 10.00–22.00 Fri–Mon & Wed, 10.00–20.00 Thur; school holidays 10.00–23.00; exhibition times may vary ⓜ Metro: Champs-Élysées Clemenceau or Franklin D. Roosevelt

Musée d'Art Moderne de la Ville de Paris

The city's modern art museum champions artists such as Steve McQueen. Next door, the **Palais de Tokyo** (① 01 47 23 54 01 ⓦ www.palaisdetokyo.com ② 12.00–21.00 Tues–Sun) showcases

PARIS MUSEUM PASS

If one of your reasons for coming to Paris is to make a lot of museum visits, the Paris Museum Pass will save you time and money. The Pass allows you to jump queues and gives unlimited access to over 60 museums and monuments. You can buy cards for two, four or six days. See ⓦ www.parismuseumpass.com for prices and details.

changing exhibitions of contemporary art. ⓐ 11 av. du Président Wilson, 16th ⓣ 01 53 67 40 00 ⓦ www.mam.paris.fr ⓛ 10.00–18.00 Tues–Sun (until 20.00 Wed for temporary exhibitions) ⓝ Metro: Iéna

Musée Dapper

This small, intimate space displays African art, from sub-Sahara to the diasporas of the continent. There is free admission on the last Wed of the month. ⓐ 35 bis rue Paul Valéry, 16th ⓣ 01 45 00 91 75 ⓦ www.dapper.com.fr ⓛ 11.00–19.00 Wed–Mon ⓝ Metro: Victor Hugo

Musée du Louvre

One of the world's largest museums, the Musée du Louvre exhibits only 10 per cent of its works. It is renowned for such masterpieces as the *Mona Lisa* (affectionately called *La Joconde* by the French), the *Venus de Milo*, *Winged Victory*, *Psyche and Cupid*, Leonardo's *Virgin and Child with St Anne* and Géricault's *Raft of the Medusa*. With some 8 departments and 35,000 works on display, the Louvre could be daunting to those trying to take in its immensity of riches. Yet rooms with polished wood floors and warm lighting are immediately inviting. The best approach is to pick a favourite period and hone in on that. You won't see it all, so relax and enjoy. The wonders that you do see will provide a lifetime of memories.

Even if you're not visiting the Louvre, you can walk through Passage Richelieu off Rue de Rivoli to view some of the museum's wondrous marble and bronze sculptures through large windows. Upon entering the central courtyard, the Cour Napoléon, you'll see I M Pei's *Pyramid* of glass and rivets. This modern structure, which is the museum's main entrance, has had many complaining that it spoilt the symmetry of the old buildings. Yet with the ancient structures reflected in the modern one and fountains further softening the transition, most visitors feel that the effect is a harmonious juxtaposition of palace and pyramid. ⓐ rue de Rivoli, 1st ⓣ 01 40 20 50 50 ⓦ www.louvre.fr ⓛ 09.00–18.00 Sat–Mon & Thur, 09.00–21.45 Wed & Fri ⓜ Metro: Palais Royal-Musée du Louvre

◬ *Even the courtyard of the Louvre is a work of art*

Musée Marmottan Monet

This lovely museum, in what was once a private home, houses a large collection of Impressionists, among other works, particularly *The Water Lilies* and other masterpieces by Monet. ⓐ 2 rue Louis-Boilly, 16th ⓣ 01 44 96 50 33 ⓦ www.marmottan.com ⓛ 10.00–20.00 Tues, 10.00–18.00 Wed–Sun ⓝ Metro: La Muette

Musée National des Arts Asiatiques-Guimet

This is one of the world's best collections of Asian art. Some 45,000 objects include works from China, Japan, India and Southeast Asia. Its annex, the **Panthéon Bouddhique** (ⓐ 19 av. d'Iéna, 16th ⓣ 01 40 73 88 00 ⓛ 09.45–17.45 Wed–Mon ⓘ Call before visiting), is a little-known jewel with ancient Buddhist statues, a Japanese garden and tea pavilion. The garden, a tiny oasis, has stands of bamboo, trickling waterfalls, wooden walkways and flowers. ⓐ 6 pl. d'Iéna, 16th ⓣ 01 56 52 53 00 ⓦ www.guimet.fr ⓛ 10.00–18.00 Wed–Mon ⓝ Metro: Iéna

Palais Garnier: Opéra National de Paris

Built on the orders of Napoleon III, the Palais Garnier, with its grand façade and foyer (both renovated in 2006), is a masterpiece of 19th-century design. It was designed by Charles Garnier to resemble a classical château. With its sweeping marble staircase, mirrors and gilded mosaics in the grand foyer, sculptures and painted ceiling depicting allegories of music, this awe-inspiring building is one of the most visited in Paris. The horseshoe-shaped auditorium has a ceiling painted by Marc Chagall. It offers a full programme of dance, ballet and opera year-round, except August. The best way to see the Opéra in action is to attend a performance – in which case do book well in advance, since popular shows are almost always sold out.

Alternatively, you can visit the staircase, foyers, auditorium (when not in use) and a small museum and exhibition hall during the day for a small fee. Guided tours are also offered in English.
🚇 pl. de l'Opéra, 2nd ☎ 08 92 89 90 90; guided tours: 08 25 05 44 05
🌐 www.operadeparis.fr ⏰ 10.00–17.00; 90-min guided tours in English: 11.30, 14.30 Wed, Sat & Sun (daily in July & Aug) Ⓜ Metro: Opéra

Petit Palais

The city's sumptuous fine arts museum contains the spectrum of art from antiquities to early 20th century. There are also excellent temporary exhibitions. 🚇 av. Winston Churchill, 8th ☎ 01 53 43 40 00
🌐 www.petitpalais.paris.fr ⏰ 10.00–18.00 Tues–Sun (until 20.00 Thur for temporary exhibitions) Ⓜ Metro: Champs-Élysées Clemenceau or Concorde

RETAIL THERAPY

The Golden Triangle of haute couture is here, extending from Rue du Faubourg Saint-Honoré, Place Vendôme and Rue Royale to Rue Montaigne and the Champs-Élysées. Fashion boutiques in Rue Étienne Marcel, in the 1st and 2nd *arrondissements*, have become recently hip with the showbiz set.

Carrousel du Louvre The inverted glass pyramid of the Louvre adds light and design drama to the Carrousel du Louvre. With its 45 boutiques and 14 restaurants, shoppers can keep occupied for hours. Goods range from fashion and jewellery to household items. Entrance on Rue de Rivoli, through the museum or the metro.
🚇 99 rue de Rivoli, 1st 🌐 www.carrouseldulouvre.com ⏰ 08.00–23.00; shops: 10.00–20.00 Ⓜ Metro: Palais Royal-Musée du Louvre

◗ *Galeries Lafayette with that special Christmas sparkle*

Colette Probably the hippest boutique in town, with accessories, bling, CDs, clothes, tech toys and trinkets for the seriously fashionable. There's a water bar downstairs with designer *eau* and a resident dog. 🚇 213 rue Saint-Honoré, 1st 📞 01 55 35 33 90 🌐 www.colette.fr 🕐 11.00–19.00 Mon–Sat 🚇 Metro: Tuileries or Pyramides

Cop Copine An original little *créateur boutique* for women that has clothes which are both comfortable and stylish. It can be a bit pricey, but you can get good discounts during the sales. There are two in Paris: 🚇 80 rue Rambuteau, 3rd 📞 01 40 28 03 72 🌐 www.cop-copine.com 🕐 10.30–19.00 Mon–Sat. Also 🚇 37 rue Étienne Marcel, 2nd 📞 01 53 00 94 80

Fauchon Taking up two corners of Place de la Madeleine and with shops all over town, Fauchon is perhaps the most elegant gourmet food store in Paris, selling fine foods from chocolates and foie gras to teas since 1886. A mini rose-coloured bag with two chocolates will give friends back home a taste of Paris. 🚇 24–26 pl. de la Madeleine, 8th 📞 01 70 39 38 00 🌐 www.fauchon.com 🕐 09.40–19.00 Mon–Sat 🚇 Metro: Madeleine

Forum des Halles A sprawling subterranean shopping and cinema complex in the 1st *arrondissement*, this place buzzes with young shoppers, but the crowds can be crushing. 🚇 101 Porte Berger 📞 01 44 76 96 56 🌐 www.forumdeshalles.com 🕐 10.00–20.00 Mon–Sat 🚇 Metro: Châtelet or Les Halles

Galeries Lafayette In the Opéra district, this elegant Parisian department store has designer togs, an activewear department, a children's 'concept store', a separate building for men and a gourmet

food section. The Lafayette Maison across the street (No 35) has everything for the home. ⓐ 40 blvd Haussmann, 9th ⓣ 01 42 82 34 56 ⓦ www.galerieslafayette.com ⓛ 09.30–20.00 Mon–Wed, Fri & Sat, 09.30–21.00 Thur ⓝ Metro: Chaussée-d'Antin-Lafayette

Marché aux Puces de la Porte de Clignancourt You can find some gems tucked among the junk at this huge flea market, which extends beyond the *périphérique* (ring road) into Saint-Ouen. ⓐ av. de la Porte de Clignancourt, 8th ⓦ www.les-puces.com ⓛ 09.00–18.00 Sat–Mon ⓝ Metro: Porte de Clignancourt or Garibaldi

Le Printemps A department store near Galeries Lafayette that also stocks a wide variety of fashionable clothes and accessories. ⓐ 64 blvd Haussmann, 9th ⓣ 01 42 82 50 00 ⓦ www.printemps.fr ⓛ 09.35–20.00 Fri–Wed, 09.35–22.00 Thur ⓝ Metro: Havre-Caumartin

Zara With some 25 locations around Paris, this Spanish clothing store has copies of catwalk fashions at affordable prices. Items for men and children too. ⓐ 2 rue Halévy, 9th ⓣ 01 44 71 90 90 ⓛ 10.00–20.00 Mon–Sat ⓝ Metro: Opéra

TAKING A BREAK

Angelina £ ❶ This elegant patisserie and tea salon has a *fin-de-siècle* dining room as frothy as the cappuccino. Its hot chocolate is legendary. ⓐ 226 rue de Rivoli, 1st ⓣ 01 42 60 82 00 ⓛ 08.00–19.00 Mon–Fri, 09.00–19.00 Sat & Sun ⓝ Metro: Tuileries

Cafés Verlet £ ❷ This cosy café features mirrors and old wood furnishings, canvas sacks of coffee beans and large old tea tins.

You can purchase tea or coffee to take away or enjoy on the premises. ② 256 rue Saint-Honoré, 1st ☎ 01 42 60 67 39 ⓦ www.cafesverlet.com ● 09.00–19.00 Mon–Sat (kitchen closes 18.00) Ⓜ Metro: Pyramides

Cojean £ ❸ Fast food is healthy food here and you can indulge in soups, sandwiches, salads and juices; everything's fresh. ② 4–6 rue de Sèze (off blvd de la Madeleine), 9th ☎ 01 40 06 08 80 ⓦ www.cojean.fr ● 08.30–18.00 Mon–Fri, 10.00–19.00 Sat Ⓜ Metro: Madeleine

Ladurée £ ❹ This celebrated tea salon (established 1862) is known for its excellent pastries and ornate dining room. It's also famous for its melt-in-your-mouth macaroons. ② 16 rue Royale, 8th ☎ 01 42 60 21 79 ⓦ www.laduree.fr ● 08.30–19.30 Mon–Thur, 08.30–20.00 Fri & Sat, 10.00–19.00 Sun Ⓜ Metro: Madeleine

Au Progrès £ ❺ A simple café and bistro in Montmartre, with friendly staff and big picture windows from which to see the spires of the Sacré-Coeur peeking above the old buildings. ② 7 rue des Trois Frères, 18th ☎ 01 42 64 07 37 ● 09.30–02.00 Ⓜ Metro: Anvers

AFTER DARK

RESTAURANTS
Le Chartier £ ❻ Since 1896, this traditional French bistro has offered standard French fare in a crowded, high-ceilinged room. The lively, old-fashioned atmosphere is the main attraction. ② 7 rue du Faubourg Montmartre, 9th ☎ 01 47 70 86 29 ⓦ www.restaurant-chartier.com ● 11.30–22.00 Ⓜ Metro: Grands Boulevards ❶ Tables cannot be booked, so you may have to queue

La Crypte de Polska £ ❼ Ever dined in the crypt of a church? This one, in the basement of a Polish church, sells such hearty Polish fare as pork and cabbage dishes at reasonable prices. Ⓐ 1 pl. Maurice Barrès, 1st ① 01 42 60 43 33 🕑 12.00–15.00, 19.30–23.00 Thur–Sat Ⓜ Metro: Pyramides

Au Vieux Châtelet £ ❽ Simple French fare at reasonable prices is offered by this traditional café-brasserie, which has a view of the river and some of the city's oldest buildings. Ⓐ 1 pl. du Châtelet (near entrance to Châtelet metro station), 1st ① 01 42 33 79 27 Ⓦ www.auvieuxchatelet.com 🕑 11.30–23.30 Ⓜ Metro: Châtelet

Café Marly ££ ❾ In the Louvre, this trendy café-restaurant serves modern fare with a view of the sculptures and the glass pyramid. Ⓐ 93 rue de Rivoli, 1st ① 01 49 26 06 60 🕑 08.00–24.00 Ⓜ Metro: Palais Royal-Musée du Louvre

Chez Cécile – La Ferme des Mathurins ££ ❿ Young chef Stéphane Pitré works wonders with unusual ingredients here, and every Thursday there's live jazz. Ⓐ 17 rue Vignon, 9th ① 01 42 66 46 39 Ⓦ www.chezcecile.com 🕑 12.15–14.00, 19.15–22.30 Mon–Fri, 19.15–22.30 Sat

La Fermette Marbeuf 1900 ££ ⓫ In this listed monument between the Champs-Élysées and the Seine, you can dine in an Art Nouveau sun lounge and enjoy perfect service and classic French cuisine. Ⓐ 5 rue Marbeuf, 8th ① 01 53 23 08 00 Ⓦ www.fermettemarbeuf.com 🕑 12.00–15.00, 19.00–23.30 Ⓜ Metro: Alma-Marceau or Franklin D Roosevelt

BARS, CLUBS & ENTERTAINMENT

Le Bar du Plaza Athénée Among the young French designers putting their distinctive stamp on Paris is Patrick Jouin, who has transformed the bar at the Hôtel Plaza Athénée into a hot nightspot with a cool idea: an 'iceberg' counter. ❸ 25 av. Montaigne, 8th ❶ 01 53 67 66 00 Ⓦ www.plaza-athenee-paris.com Ⓛ 18.00–02.00 Ⓜ Metro: Alma-Marceau or Franklin D. Roosevelt

Charlie Birdy The Charlie Birdy chain has several addresses in Paris, and they provide a popular blend of American bar and British pub, with a Soul and Jazz Brunch from noon on Sundays. ❸ 124 rue La Boétie, 8th ❶ 01 42 25 18 06 Ⓦ www.charliebirdy.com Ⓛ 09.00–05.00 Ⓜ Metro: Franklin D. Roosevelt

Le Divan du Monde A great name ('the world's divan') for a great place that offers all styles of music and shows. ❸ 75 rue des Martyrs, 9th ❶ 01 40 05 06 99 Ⓦ www.divandumonde.com Ⓛ 19.00–03.00 Ⓜ Metro: Pigalle

Le Duc des Lombards One of this music-loving city's best jazz clubs attracts aficionados with its big-name performers. You can also eat here. ❸ 42 rue des Lombards, 4th ❶ 01 42 33 22 88 Ⓦ www.ducdeslombards.com Ⓛ Concerts usually 20.00 or 22.00–24.00 Mon–Sat (until 03.00 or 04.00 Sat after jam session) Ⓜ Metro: Châtelet

Rex Club This popular club is great for hardcore dancers who like shaking to house, techno and electro. ❸ 5 blvd Poissonnière, 2nd ❶ 01 42 36 10 96 Ⓦ www.rexclub.com Ⓛ 23.30–06.00 Wed–Sat Ⓜ Metro: Bonne Nouvelle

Right Bank East

The Right Bank East is the oldest part of Paris, including Île de la Cité, Île Saint-Louis and the Marais. Much of it was untouched by the great modernisation of the 1860s, so here you still find ancient cobbled streets, small courtyards and medieval buildings that appear to sag and lean into the street. Its 10th, 19th and 20th *arrondissements* are called 'the people's Paris', while the Marais and the Bastille are hip; Bastille, particularly, hums with bars and clubs. The main attractions include the Notre-Dame cathedral, the Marais district, Canal Saint-Martin, the Bastille area with its modern opera house, and Père-Lachaise cemetery.

SIGHTS & ATTRACTIONS

Bastille

The column in the centre of Place de la Bastille, topped by a golden liberty statue, is the symbol of the French Revolution. It was here, in 1789, that the people of Paris stormed the Bastille prison, freeing the prisoners and rising in arms against the excesses of the aristocrats and the royalty. The 51.5-m (nearly 170-ft) Colonne de Juillet commemorates the victims of two subsequent uprisings (in 1830 and 1848), who are buried in the crypt at its base. People still rally here today during major demonstrations. The metro station's brightly painted tiles depict scenes from the uprisings.

Today, the Bastille district in the 11th is a lively people place, with the modern Opéra Bastille and the streets surrounding the square providing a party atmosphere, especially at night and on weekends. Among the trendy clubs off the square is OPA (see page 97). ⓜ Metro: Bastille

Right Bank East

500 metres
500 yards

Barbès
Rochechouart

La Chapelle

Stalingrad

Musée de la Musique

Avenue Jean-Jaurès

Parc de la Villette & Cité des Sciences

Gare du Nord

Louis Blanc

Jaurès

Riquet

Bolívar

Parc des Buttes Chaumont

RUE DE MAGENTA

Gare du Nord

10e

Château-Landon

RUE DU PLATEAU

Buttes Chaumont

Poissonnière

Gare de l'Est

Gare de l'Est

Colonel Fabien

AVENUE MATHURIN MOREAU

BOULEVARD DE LA VILLETTE

RUE DE CHABROL

Square Villemin

Hôtel du Nord

RUE DE BELLEVILLE

Belleville

Parc de Belleville

BD DE MAGENTA

Jacques-Bonsergent

Couronnes

Strasbourg Saint-Denis

BD SAINT-MARTIN

RUE DU FAUBOURG DU TEMPLE

Goncourt

Ménilmontant

Musée des Arts et Métiers

PLACE DE LA RÉPUBLIQUE

Temple

République

Parmentier

Institut de Management Europe-Paris

RUE RÉAUMUR

Arts et Métiers

AVENUE DE LA RÉPUBLIQUE

Oberkampf

BOULEVARD DE LA VILLETTE

Cimetière du Père-Lachaise

3e

Filles du Calvaire

St-Sébastien Froissart

Musée de la Poupée

Musée d'Art et d'Histoire du Judaïsme

Musée de la Chasse et de la Nature

Saint-Ambroise

Rambuteau

Centre Pompidou

Musée de l'Histoire de France

Richard Lenoir

Marché Richard Lenoir

Voltaire

BEAUBOURG

MARAIS

Bréguet Sabin

11e

RUE DE LA ROQUETTE

Hôtel de Ville

Hôtel de Ville

RIVOLI

Saint-Paul

Voltaire

Maison Européenne de la Photographie

Maison de Victor Hugo

PLACE DES VOSGES

ÎLE DE LA CITÉ

Pont Marie

QUAI DES CELESTINS

PLACE DE LA BASTILLE

Bastille

Notre-Dame

QUAI DE LA TOURNELLE

ÎLE SAINT-LOUIS

Sully-Morland

Opéra Bastille

Ledru-Rollin

Flower & bird market

Préfecture de Paris

BD HENRI IV

RUE DU FAUBOURG SAINT-ANTOINE

Institut du Monde Arabe

Cardinal Lemoine

Universités Paris VI Pierre et Marie Curie Paris VII Denis Diderot

Jussieu

5e

Jardin des Plantes

La Cinémathèque Française & Bercy Village

Gare de Lyon

Gare de Lyon

BOULEVARD DIDEROT

POI
Metro Stop
Cathedral
Information
Police Station
Railway Stn
Hospital

Canal cruise

A different way to look at Paris is from a canal boat. The leisurely, two-and-a-half-hour cruise on the Canal Saint-Martin passes through numerous locks, under footbridges and along a 595-m (⅓-mile) vault of the Bastille, with the Japanese artist Keiichi Tahara's *Sounds of Light* laser light show dancing along the tunnel walls. The day-long tour to the Marne River goes to the 'land of *guinguettes*' (riverside open-air dance clubs) and rural France. **Canauxrama** runs tours most days through the summer, but check with the company for a current schedule. Tours start from the Bastille's Port de l'Arsenal,

🔺 *View from a canal*

a giant marina accommodating 200 boats, near the Bastille metro station. ⓐ Office: Bassin de la Villette, 13 quai de la Loire, 19th
ⓣ 01 42 39 15 00 ⓦ www.canauxrama.com ⓛ 09.45, 14.30 (Apr–Sept); by reservation other times; call for dinner cruise times
ⓜ Metro: Bastille (departure point) or Jaurès (office)

Canal Saint-Martin

With pedestrian quays on both sides (Valmy and Jemmapes), Canal Saint-Martin is a pleasant waterway meandering from Place de la République to the La Villette basin. Little boutiques, bistros and cafés have made this promenade popular with walkers, cyclists and rollerbladers. The **Hôtel du Nord** (ⓐ 102 quai de Jemmapes, 10th
ⓣ 01 40 40 78 78 ⓦ www.hoteldunord.org), where the film of the same name was filmed, is now a trendy restaurant and bar. ⓜ Metro: République (pl. de la République) or Jaurès (Bassin de la Villette)

Cimetière du Père-Lachaise

Paris's first secular cemetery is now one of its most visited sights. Among the famous figures buried here are Molière, Apollinaire, Chopin, Modigliani, Proust and Oscar Wilde. Jim Morrison fans flock to his tomb in a never-ending pilgrimage. An elaborate, life-sized reclining bronze statue of playboy journalist Victor Noir, shot in a duel on 10 January, 1870, has become a fertility symbol, his prominent tumescence polished to a bright shine by generations of hopeful women. With its tree-lined alleys and flowers, the Père-Lachaise is like a garden, with 44 ha (109 acres) of greenery amid the tombs. There are guided visits in English during July and August (call ⓣ 01 71 28 50 82 to book). ⓐ 16 rue du Repos, 20th ⓣ 01 55 25 82 10 ⓛ 08.00–17.30 Mon–Fri, 08.30–17.30 Sat, 09.00–17.30 Sun (until 18.00 daily in summer)
ⓜ Metro: Père-Lachaise

Île Saint-Louis

Right behind Notre-Dame, Île Saint-Louis is actually made up of two islets that joined together in 1614. Laundry women once worked here, but now only the quayside façades remain, and Rue Saint-Louis-en-l'Île evokes that earlier era. Below, on hot summer days, sunbathers stretch out and impromptu parties occur. On the opposite banks, *bouquinistes* sell their second-hand books, postcards and posters. Ⓝ Metro: Pont-Marie

Le Marais

One of the city's oldest areas, the Marais (a marsh drained to make aristocrats' mansions in the 16th century) is an intimate area of speciality boutiques, restaurants and museums. The district is great for strolling, with its narrow streets, ancient timbered houses, cobbled cloisters, fountains, squares, surprising architectural details including a mosaic-covered building and houses so aged they lean into the street. Many Marais shops, particularly on Rue des Francs Bourgeois, are open on Sunday. Ⓝ Metro: Saint-Paul

Notre-Dame

With its dusky white towers rising above the Île de la Cité in the centre of the Seine, the Notre-Dame cathedral, a Gothic masterpiece, is one of the best-loved sights in Paris. Victor Hugo immortalised the cathedral in his novel *Notre-Dame de Paris*. The French version of the film of the book (1957) has wonderful scenes of the hunchback and the gypsy Esmeralda on the balcony of the towers, with jutting gargoyles and views of Paris. Tower visits are free on the first Sunday of the month.

Directly in front of the cathedral, and overlooked by many sightseers, a staircase leads down to the archaeological Crypt of the Parvis of Notre-Dame, housing vestiges of earlier civilisations, from Gallo-Roman to the 19th century. They were first discovered during excavations in the 1960s. The largest structure of its type in the world, it extends 118 m (387 ft).

Often unnoticed, a brass plaque in the stones of the *parvis* (square) in front of the Notre-Dame marks kilometre zero. Distances to various destinations in France are marked from that point. ❸ 6 Parvis de Notre-Dame, Île de la Cité, 4th ❶ 01 53 10 07 00 ❿ www.monum.fr or www.notredamedeparis.fr ❶ Tower: 10.00–18.30 summer; 10.00–17.30 winter (until 23.00 Sat & Sun June–Aug); cathedral: 08.00–18.45 Mon–Fri, 08.00–19.15 Sat & Sun; free guided visits in English: 14.00 Wed & Thur, 14.30 Sat ❿ Metro: St-Michel or Cité

Parc des Buttes Chaumont

This charming park perched above an eastern Parisian hill in the 19th *arrondissement* has artificial rivers, caves and cascades, as well as a folly in the shape of a Greco-Roman temple. It was built to encourage relaxation, and kids will love the ducks, Punch and Judy puppet show and the pony rides! ❶ 07.00–22.00 (summer); 07.00–21.00 (winter) ❿ Metro: Botzaris or Buttes Chaumont

Parc de la Villette

Park, concert venue, cultural complex, La Villette is all these rolled into one lively, entertaining destination. The 28-ha (69-acre) urban park has everything from a bamboo grove to sprawling lawns where an open-air summer cinema festival takes place (see page 9). In the spherical Géode, a huge, hemispheric screen shows IMAX films. La Villette also includes the Cité des Sciences (see pages 88–9) and the Musée de la Musique (see page 90). ❶ 01 40 03 75 75 ❿ www.villette.com ❿ Metro: Porte de Pantin or Porte de la Villette

Place de la République

Along with the Bastille, Place de la République is known as a place for partying. A giant bronze statue representing the French Republic stands at its centre. Ⓜ Metro: République

CULTURE

Centre Pompidou

Whatever you may think of the industrial chic look, this is France's most important modern art museum, showcasing the world's greatest 20th- and 21st-century artists. You can see great views from its top floor and the **Georges** restaurant (Ⓣ 01 44 78 47 99 ⓘ Reservations recommended). On the first Sunday of the month admission to the exhibitions is free. Place Beaubourg in front of the Centre Pompidou is an animated gathering place, with musicians and other performers amusing the crowds, so you can enjoy this destination even if you don't wish to art-gaze. Tip: to avoid queuing, visit the museum after 17.00. Ⓐ pl. Georges Pompidou, 4th Ⓣ 01 44 78 12 33 Ⓦ www.centrepompidou.fr Ⓛ 11.00–21.00 Wed–Mon (until 23.00 Thur for some temporary exhibitions); last entry one hour before closing Ⓜ Metro: Rambuteau

La Cinémathèque Française

This treasure trove of cinema history includes an exceptional collection of 40,000 films plus a film-themed library, exhibition halls and four cinema theatres showing classic films from all types of cinema year-round. Ⓐ 51 rue de Bercy, Parc de Bercy, 12th Ⓣ 01 71 19 33 33 Ⓦ www.cinematheque.fr Ⓛ 12.00–19.00 Mon & Wed–Sat, 10.00–20.00 Sun Ⓜ Metro: Bercy

◆ The funky Georges restaurant at Centre Pompidou

Cité des Sciences

Part of the Parc de la Villette, the excellent Cité des Sciences (housed in a former abattoir) hosts fascinating exhibitions relating to science, technology and the natural world, including many hands-on experiments. There are frequent guided tours and workshops, plus two special sections dedicated to children aged 2–5 and 5–12. There is also a planetarium and IMAX cinema, with headphones

⬤ *The eye-catching Géode IMAX cinema at the Cité des Sciences*

NIGHT VIEWS

All of the Seine's bridges are illuminated at night, so anywhere you walk along the river you get that quintessential romantic Paris perspective. Diners at the Bistro Marguerite (see pages 94–5) get splendid night views of the Seine right across the street, with perhaps the moon lighting the scene from above. Across Place de l'Hôtel de Ville, the grand Town Hall is spotlit at night and glows beside the Seine.

giving commentary in English. ⓐ 30 av. Corentin-Cariou, 19th ⓣ 01 40 05 70 00 ⓦ www.cite-sciences.fr ⓛ 09.30–18.00 Tues–Sat, 09.30–19.00 Sun ⓜ Metro: Porte de la Villette

Maison Européenne de la Photographie

This gallery supports major contemporary figures working in exhibition prints, the printed page and film. ⓐ 5–7 rue de Fourcy, 4th ⓣ 01 44 78 75 00 ⓦ www.mep-fr.org ⓛ 11.00–20.00 Wed–Sun ⓜ Metro: Saint-Paul or Pont Marie

Musée des Arts et Métiers

This fascinating museum dedicated to inventions and technology from the 16th century to today houses some 80,000 objects. Exhibits include steam-powered vehicles, such as Cugnot's Fardier, and planes flown by Blériot and Ader. The building, an ancient priory, is particularly appealing. Even the metro station is inventive (on line 11 only, not line 3), resembling the inside of a copper-toned submarine. ⓐ 60 rue Réaumur, 3rd ⓣ 01 53 01 82 00 ⓦ www.arts-et-metiers.net ⓛ 10.00–18.00 Tues, Wed & Fri–Sun, 10.00–21.30 Thur ⓜ Metro: Arts et Métiers

Musée de la Musique

Featuring a 900-year history of musical instruments, the museum is part of the Cité de la Musique, which houses several concert halls, a music school and the Paris Conservatoire in the Parc de la Villette. It displays scale models of musical venues and opera houses as well as instrument collections dating back to the Middle Ages. ⓐ 221 av. Jean Jaurès, 19th ⓣ 01 44 84 44 84 ⓦ www.cite-musique.fr ⓛ 12.00–18.00 Tues–Sat, 10.00–18.00 Sun ⓝ Metro: Porte de Pantin

Opéra Bastille

Designed by Carlos Ott and opened in 1989 for the bicentenary of the French Revolution, the curved, glass-fronted Opéra Bastille has transformed the face of the Bastille district. A full programme of opera and dance is available throughout the year (except August). The building is known for its excellent acoustics – all the better to hear the singers' bel canto. ⓐ pl. de la Bastille, 12th ⓣ 08 92 89 90 90 ⓦ www.operadeparis.fr ⓝ Metro: Bastille

RETAIL THERAPY

Alternatives This tiny boutique in the Marais features couture cast-offs (mainly for men) from such designers as Gucci, Issy Miyake and Jean-Paul Gaultier. ⓐ 18 rue du Roi de Sicile, 4th ⓣ 01 42 78 31 50 ⓛ 13.00–19.00 Tues–Fri, by appointment Sat ⓝ Metro: Saint-Paul

Antoine & Lili Local clothing designers have created a hit line of reasonably priced clothes and accessories for women in Antoine & Lili. Stores in bright pinks, yellows and greens are cheerful and fun. Several locations around Paris, the biggest being: ⓐ 95 quai de Valmy, 10th ⓣ 01 40 37 41 55 ⓦ www.antoineetlili.com ⓛ 11.00–19.00

🔺 *The modern architecture of the Opéra Bastille*

Sun & Mon, 11.00–20.00 Tues–Sat Ⓜ Metro: Jacques Bonsergent.
Also ⓐ 51 rue des Francs Bourgeois, 4th ☎ 01 42 72 26 60 Ⓜ Metro:
Hôtel de Ville

Bercy Village Shopping, dining and relaxing in a riverside atmosphere
are all here at the Cour Saint-Émilion in Bercy Village. This is not
just a commercial venture. People live in this engaging complex
that was once the world's largest wine market. There is even a
bakery school. ⓐ 28 rue François Truffaut, 12th ☎ 01 40 02 90 80
Ⓦ www.bercyvillage.com 🕐 07.00–02.00; shops: 11.00–21.00;
restaurants: 11.00–02.00 Ⓜ Metro: Cour Saint-Émilion

CSAO The spacious Compagnie du Sénégal et de l'Afrique de l'Ouest
reflects Paris's rich African population, promoting the best of Senegal

⬤ *A great choice of bird boxes at the lively Sunday bird market*

in this cheerful shop with its 'sustainably minded' accessories and trinkets. Bright little plastic bracelets resembling beaded bangles are a modern version of the old elephant hair bracelets Senegalese ladies wore. Rhythmic African CDs, paintings, baskets aplenty, funky furniture from recycled materials and calabash gourd bowls are all sold. ⓐ 9 rue Elzévir, 3rd ⓣ 01 42 71 33 17 ⓦ www.csao.fr ⓛ 14.00–19.00 Sun & Mon, 11.00–19.00 Tue–Sat ⓜ Metro: Saint-Paul

Flower & bird market The flower market is a sight to behold with its array of colourful and aromatic flora. On Sundays, songbirds, cockatoos and other feathered friends are also sold here. ⓐ pl. Louis-Lépine,

Île de la Cité, 4th 🕒 Flower market: 08.00–19.30; bird market: 08.00–19.00 Sun only Ⓜ Metro: Cité

Marché Richard Lenoir North from Place de la Bastille, this wonderful market is one of the best in the city, attracting food suppliers from far and wide. It's a great place to spend Sunday mornings, provided you're hungry. 🕒 09.00–13.00 Thur & Sun Ⓜ Métro: Bastille

Place des Vosges The arcades around the beautiful, historic Place des Vosges are lined with gallery upon gallery of modern and classical art. Well worth a browse even if you're not able to face the price tags. There are plenty of cafés too. Ⓜ Metro: Saint-Paul or Bastille

Viaduc des Arts A renovated train viaduct has metamorphosed into a clutch of craftsmen's shops and showrooms at the Viaduc des Arts. Above is as delightful a surprise as the brick boutiques below. Here, the elevated Promenade Plantée, a flowering footpath linking several gardens, winds nearly 5 km (3 miles) along an old railway line to the Bois de Vincennes. The peaceful urban 'lung' provides a great, unobstructed view of the 12th *arrondissement*. Ⓦ www.viaducdesarts.fr Ⓜ Metro: Bastille

TAKING A BREAK

Le Bar à Thé £ ❶ Cosy tea room that serves every type of tea you can imagine; perfect to accompany one of their delicious home-made cakes or desserts. ⓐ 9 rue Antoine Vollon, 12th ☎ 01 43 40 90 17 Ⓦ www.barathe.fr 🕒 10.00–18.30 Wed–Sun Ⓜ Metro: Ledru-Rollin

Berthillon £ ② Even on rainy, cold days there is a queue at Berthillon, the city's finest ice-cream shop. Choose from around 40 exotic flavours. ⓐ 29–31 rue Saint-Louis-en-l'Île, 4th ① 01 43 54 31 61 ⓦ www.berthillon.fr ⓛ 10.00–20.00 Wed–Sun ⓝ Metro: Pont Marie

Chez Prune £ ③ A cheerful little bar-restaurant with mango-yellow walls and a slightly worn look. Staff are very friendly and there's a lively buzz. ⓐ 71 quai de Valmy, 10th ① 01 42 41 30 47 ⓛ 08.00–02.00 Mon–Sat, from 10.00 Sun ⓝ Metro: Goncourt or Jacques Bonsergent

Le Pain Quotidien £ ④ You can eat indoors or out in the café of this popular bakery, with healthy salads, indulgent pastries and delicious little *tartines*. ⓐ 18–20 rue des Archives, 4th ① 01 44 54 03 07 ⓛ 08.00–22.00 daily ⓝ Metro: Hôtel-de-Ville

Sacha Finkelsztajn £ ⑤ The sign on Sacha Finkelsztajn's window reads 'Gastronomie Europe Centrale et Russie'. Polish immigrants founded the original store here in 1851, and now it sells such specialities as cheesecake, huge cinnamon-sprinkled apple strudels and just-baked bread. Deli items include traditional sausages, dill pickles and salads. ⓐ 27 rue des Rosiers, 4th ① 01 42 72 78 91 ⓦ http://finkelsztajn.com ⓛ 10.00–19.00 Wed–Mon (mid-Aug–mid-July) ⓝ Metro: Saint-Paul

AFTER DARK

RESTAURANTS

Le Bistro Marguerite £ ⑥ This Seine-side gem, with its view of the Hôtel de Ville and riverside setting, is a typical French bistro with a rustic, country décor, friendly staff and reasonable prices. Choices include such traditional French fare as *aligot* (puréed cheese and garlic potatoes) and tender pork knuckle. Also open for breakfast and lunch. ⓐ 2 quai de Gesvres, 4th ⓣ 01 42 72 00 04 ⓛ 08.00–22.00 ⓝ Metro: Hôtel de Ville

Point Éphémère £ ❼ A trendy restaurant, bar and concert venue by the Canal Saint-Martin – perfect for a lazy lunch or weekend brunch. ⓐ 200 quai de Valmy, 10th ⓣ 01 40 34 02 48 ⓦ www.pointephemere.org ⓛ Restaurant: 12.00–14.30, 20.00–23.00; bar: 12.00–02.00 (until 21.00 Sun) ⓝ Metro: Jaurès or Stalingrad

Le Coude Fou £–££ ❽ With its naive paintings on the walls and ceiling, this quirky wine bar-restaurant serves good, typically French food with a wide choice of wines. ⓐ 12 rue du Bourg-Tibourg (off rue de Rivoli), 4th ⓣ 01 42 77 15 16 ⓛ 12.00–24.00 (kitchen: 12.00–14.45, 19.30–24.00) ⓝ Metro: Hôtel de Ville

Café de l'Industrie ££ ❾ This bar and restaurant attracts a youthful crowd with its good food at reasonable prices. Lamb noisettes and fresh fish are typical menu items. Staff are young and enthusiastic and décor is 'anthropological', with old colonial outpost photos, masks and fan palms. ⓐ 16 & 17 rue Saint-Sabin, 11th ⓣ 01 47 00 13 53 ⓛ 10.00–02.00 ⓝ Metro: Bastille

La Tête Ailleurs ££ ❿ In an old building in the Marais, this restaurant has been gentrified to provide a warm, Provençal farmhouse atmosphere. The food is excellent and the service friendly. ⓐ 20 rue Beautreillis, 4th ⓣ 01 42 72 47 80 ⓦ www.lateteailleurs.fr ⓛ 20.00–22.30 Mon & Sat, 12.00–14.00, 20.00–22.30 Tues–Fri; closed 2 wks in Aug ⓝ Metro: Saint-Paul

Le Train Bleu ££ (set menu) **£££** (à la carte) ⓫ With its belle époque ceiling hung with chandeliers and painted with scenes of Paris and other cities, this grand restaurant and its Big Ben Bar evoke a gentler age. Situated above the Gare de Lyon, which was built for the 1900 World Fair, the dining room is the best-preserved part of the original building. The restaurant attracts a mixed clientele: young locals, travellers and older Parisians. As its brochure says, outside in the modern world, 'linear design has triumphed over the curves of Baroque art'. Even if you don't wish to have a drink or a meal, it is worth popping your head in to catch a glimpse of this splendid setting. ⓐ Gare de Lyon, pl. Louis Armand, 12th ⓣ 01 44 75 76 76 ⓦ www.le-train-bleu.com ⓛ 11.30–15.00, 19.00–23.00 ⓜ Metro: Gare de Lyon

🔺 *The opulent Le Train Blue above the Gare de Lyon*

BARS, CLUBS & ENTERTAINMENT

Barrio Latino Within a magnificent steel structure designed by Eiffel himself, this salsa joint plays Latin rhythms late into the night. Also has a restaurant. ⓐ 46–48 rue du Faubourg Saint-Antoine, 12th ⓣ 01 55 78 84 75 ⓦ www.buddhabar.com ⓛ 12.00–02.00 Mon–Sat; brunch: 12.00–16.00 Sun

Bercy Live concerts are held just about every night here, with a whole range of music, including jazz, rock, hip hop and rhythm-and-blues. There's also an ice rink. ⓐ 12 blvd du Bercy, 12th ⓣ 08 92 39 01 00 ⓦ www.bercy.fr Ice rink: 15.00–18.00 Wed, 21.30–00.30 Fri, 15.00–18.00, 21.30–00.30 Sat, 10.00–12.00, 15.00–18.00 Sun; event times vary ⓜ Metro: Bercy

Flèche d'Or Café A cavernous space in a former train station, popular for its pop-rock and electro music. Music ranges from Afro and reggae to rock, jazz and rhythm-and-blues, among other genres. You have to queue to get in, and you take your chances with the music. ⓐ 102 bis rue de Bagnolet, 20th ⓣ 01 44 64 01 02 ⓦ www.flechedor.fr ⓜ Metro: Alexandre Dumas or Gambetta

New Morning A former printing shop, this Paris institution is known for its concerts of jazz and world music. ⓐ 7–9 rue des Petites-Écuries, 10th ⓣ 01 45 23 51 41 ⓦ www.newmorning.com ⓛ 20.00–01.30 Mon–Sat ⓜ Metro: Château d'Eau

OPA This nightclub offers free entry to live music, electro, rock and other sounds. ⓐ 9 rue Biscornet, 12th ⓣ 01 46 28 12 90 ⓦ www.opa-paris.com ⓛ Club: 24.00–06.00 Fri & Sat; Café-Concert: 20.00–02.00 Wed & Thur ⓜ Metro: Bastille

Left Bank

The Left Bank is the Paris of universities and bohemia, of literary cafés, student hangouts and artists' ateliers and galleries. Such historically important buildings as the Sorbonne, the Panthéon, the Eiffel Tower and the Musée d'Orsay are all found here. Although they are located on islands in the Seine, Notre-Dame and the Conciergerie are actually in the 1st *arrondissement*, and so are listed under the Right Bank. Called the *Rive Gauche* in French, the large and varied Left Bank of Paris includes the legendary Latin Quarter in the 5th *arrondissement*, the more bourgeois 7th, where the Eiffel Tower and Invalides stand, and the soaring Tour Montparnasse in the 15th.

SIGHTS & ATTRACTIONS

Boulevard Saint-Germain
While the Champs-Élysées is the grand thoroughfare of the Right Bank, Saint-Germain is the main boulevard of the Left, where boutiques and bistros, cafés and cinemas, street entertainers and *flâneurs* (strollers) all converge. It is also known for its little jazz joints and art galleries on side streets such as Rue de Seine, Rue des Beaux-Arts and Rue Bonaparte.

Église Saint-Sulpice
This fine church is noted for its paintings by Eugène Delacroix (first chapel on the right as you enter) and for its organ. The fountain square in front is a popular place to rest and often has an outdoor photo exhibition. ❸ pl. Saint-Sulpice, 6th ❶ 01 46 33 21 78
ⓦ www.paroisse-saint-sulpice-paris.org ❹ 07.30–19.30
Ⓜ Metro: Saint-Sulpice

Left Bank

0   500 metres
0   500 yards

Legend:
POI
Metro Stop
Cathedral
Information
Police Station
Railway Stn
Hospital

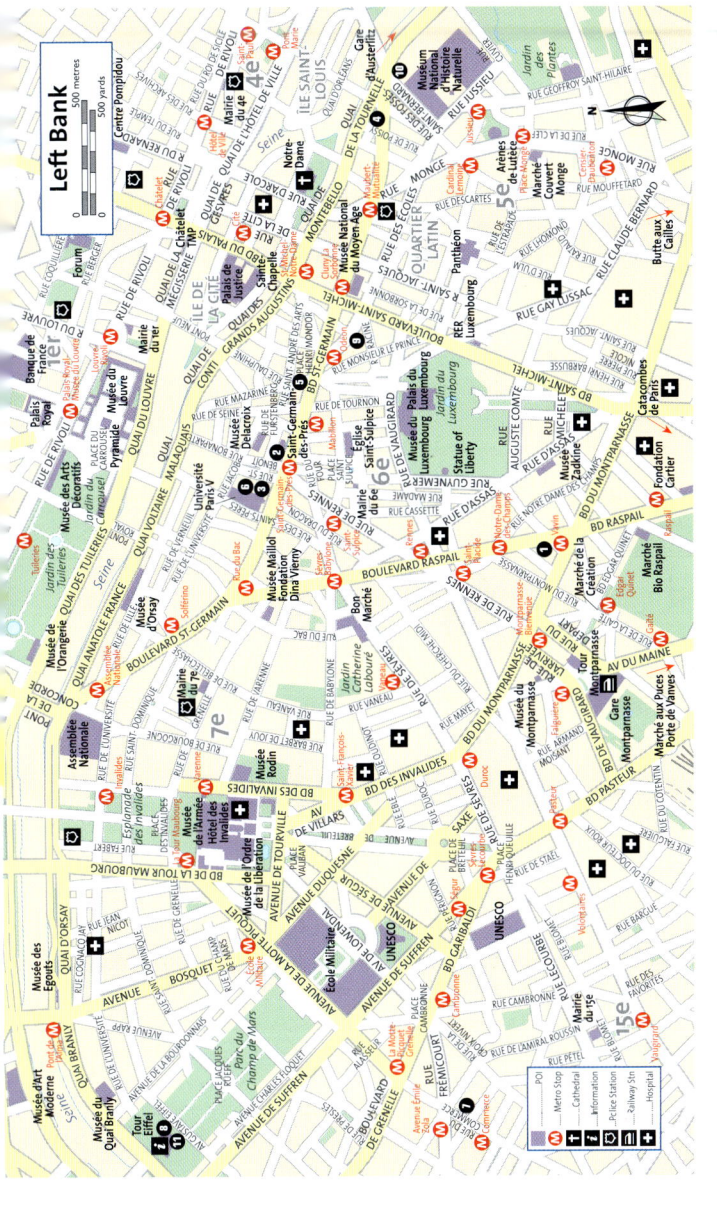

Hôtel des Invalides

Recognisable for its gold-leaf dome shining brilliantly along the Left Bank horizon, the Hôtel des Invalides is where Napoleon is buried. His ashes are protected in a sarcophagus containing six coffins, of iron, lead and wood. One of the most beautiful 17th-century monuments in Paris, Les Invalides was built during the time of Louis XIV to house wounded soldiers. Parts of it are still used as a hospital. There are five museums here, including the **Musée de l'Armée**. This is a huge collection of over half a million items, spread over several floors, and you don't need to be interested in the army to appreciate its historical importance. Its Cathédrale Saint-Louis occasionally has classical music concerts. ❸ esplanade des Invalides, 7th ❶ 08 10 11 33 99 ❿ www. invalides.org ❶ 10.00–18.00 summer (until 19.00 for the dome); 10.00–17.00 winter; closed first Mon of month ❿ Metro: Invalides

Jardin du Luxembourg

Adjacent to the Senate building, this is a true Parisian park, with an orderly French garden, tree-lined alleys, green spaces, statues and *bassins* (ponds), around which Parisians sit on fine days. The Théâtre des Marionettes (a puppet theatre) entertains children as it has done for centuries. You can watch regulars playing boules, bridge and chess, or just hang out like the locals, lounging on the metal chairs watching children sail miniature boats on the ornamental pond. A hidden charm in the west side of the Jardin du Luxembourg is the bronze model of the **Statue of Liberty**, which the sculptor Auguste Bartholdi gave to the garden in 1900 for the World Fair. Bartholdi, who sculpted the full-sized Statue of Liberty that now stands in New York harbour, based his masterpiece on this model and a larger one that fronts the Pont de Grenelle in the Seine. ❸ rue de Vaugirard, 6th ❶ Dawn–dusk ❿ RER B: Luxembourg

⬤ *The striking Hôtel des Invalides is the burial site of Napoleon*

Jardin des Plantes

Part of the natural history museum (see page 112) and dating back to a 17th-century medicinal garden, the Jardin des Plantes has one of the most beautiful rose gardens in Paris, with some 350 varieties. There are also alpine and tropical gardens, medicinal plants, as well as a micro-zoo and menagerie. ⓐ Entrance on rue Cuvier, 5th ⓣ 01 40 79 56 01 ⓛ 07.30–20.00 ⓝ Metro: Jussieu

Markets

Paris's markets are an attraction in themselves, reminiscent of the traditional form of country commerce, where vendors call out their wares to passers-by and goods range from fresh, tempting foodstuffs to books, birds and collectibles.

Marché Bio Raspail Organic food market. ⓐ blvd Raspail (between rue du Cherche Midi and Rue de Rennes), 6th ⓛ 09.00–15.00 Sun ⓝ Metro: Rennes

Marché de la Création Vendors at Montparnasse's outdoor market display a wide variety of arts, crafts and also junk. ⓐ From blvd Quinet to Montparnasse Tower, 15th ⓦ www.marchecreation.com ⓛ 10.00–dusk Sun ⓝ Metro: Edgar Quinet

Marché Couvert Monge At this covered food market in the Latin Quarter, vocal vendors sell a wide range of produce, meat, cheese and delicacies. ⓐ pl. Monge, 5th ⓛ 07.00–14.30 Wed & Fri, 07.00–15.00 Sun ⓝ Metro: Place Monge

Marché aux Puces de la Porte de Vanves Past the polyester clothing stalls and oddball junk, you can find some gems at this flea market, such as lace fabrics, antique tables and silverware. ⓐ av. Georges Lafenestre & av. Marc Sangnier, 14th ⓣ 06 86 89 99 96 ⓦ http://pucesdevanves.typepad.com ⓛ 07.00–15.00 or 17.00 Sat & Sun ⓝ Metro: Porte de Vanves

Odéon

The Odéon district of Boulevard Saint-Germain is always full of students, shoppers and film-goers (there are several major cinema complexes here). Shops range from couture to little boutiques and there are also theatres, bookshops and cafés, including Paris's oldest café, Le Procope (see page 115). Ⓜ Metro: Odéon

Panthéon

One of the most recognised of Paris monuments is the Panthéon, in the 5th *arrondissement*. Since 1791, this stately, domed structure has been the revered resting place of some of France's most eminent figures, including Voltaire, Victor Hugo, Jean-Jacques Rousseau, Émile Zola, Marie Curie and a recent inductee, Alexandre Dumas. Tours of the nave and crypt are available. A fascinating permanent exhibit is that of Foucault's pendulum, which hangs from high above in the dome's crown and swings slowly and hypnotically by observers near the Panthéon floor. Ⓐ pl. du Panthéon, 5th ❶ Guided visits in English: 01 44 54 19 30 Ⓦ www.monum.fr Ⓛ 10.00–18.30 summer; 10.00–18.00 winter Ⓜ Metro: Cardinal Lemoine or RER B: Luxembourg

Quartier Latin (Latin Quarter)

So-named because the students and teachers of the Sorbonne spoke Latin until the French Revolution (1789), the Latin Quarter in the 5th *arrondissement* has long been associated with students, writers and intellectuals. It has now expanded beyond a centre of learning to become a *quartier* of cafés and bars, boutiques, bistros and nightspots. The area includes the lively Saint-Michel warren of cobbled streets and restaurants, the Sorbonne, the Panthéon and the medieval Cluny museum. Bustling and narrow, Rue Mouffetard

is one of the city's oldest streets; it was the main road from Paris (then called Lutèce) to Rome in ancient times. 'Le Mouff' has a lively weekend market, little boutiques and reasonably priced restaurants. There is even a Roman arena, the **Arènes de Lutèce** (🚇 47 rue Monge, 5th

🔺 *A cruise along the Seine will take you past the city's best sights*

🕐 08.00–22.00 (summer); 08.00–17.30 (winter) Ⓜ Metro: Place Monge), an admission-free Gallo-Roman ruin, which was once a circus amphitheatre.

Saint-Germain-des-Prés

This Romanesque church on the boulevard bearing its name has the oldest belfry in Paris. Inside it is very peaceful, a wonderful place to ponder. On the corner of the Boulevard Saint-Germain are the legendary literary cafés Les Deux Magots and Café de Flore (see pages 113–14). 🕐 Daily (visiting & service times vary) Ⓜ Metro: Saint-Germain-des-Prés

Seine

The city was first settled on an island (the Île de la Cité) on the Seine, and the river remains one of its most appealing and vital features. Many of the city's finest attractions are found along its banks: the Louvre, Musée d'Orsay, the Eiffel Tower, Notre-Dame and the Conciergerie. The Seine can be appreciated on a stroll along its quays with its 37 distinctive bridges, or from one of the many cruise boats. Especially romantic are night-time dinner cruises.

Bâteaux Parisiens depart from the foot of the Eiffel Tower every half-hour from 10.00 to 22.30 in summer and hourly from 10.00 to 22.00 in winter. Lunch and dinner cruises are also available. ☎ 08 25 01 01 01 🌐 www.bateauxparisiens.com

Batobus, a regular boat service making eight stops along the Seine, is like an inexpensive cruise, without the commentary. Service operates year-round except January and gives great views of some of Paris's most famous buildings. ☎ 08 25 05 01 01 🌐 www.batobus.com 🕐 10.00–16.30 or 21.00 depending on season

Tour Eiffel (Eiffel Tower)

Gustave Eiffel built Paris's most visible and well-known site and the international symbol of France, the graceful Tour Eiffel, for the 1889 World Fair. When it was first assembled, the tower was widely disparaged. Parisians called it a pitiful lamppost and a hollow candlestick. Today, the French, and visitors from around the world, admire the filigreed, A-shaped structure above the Seine. At 324 m high (1,063 ft), the tower has 1,665 steps and requires some 50 tonnes of paint to repaint it in 'Tour Eiffel Brown'. Twenty thousand light bulbs light it like a birthday sparkler each hour after dark until 01.00. There are lifts to the three levels, which cost more the higher you go. If you're feeling strong (or poor), take the stairs. ❸ Champs de Mars, 7th ❶ 01 44 11 23 23 Ⓦ www.tour-eiffel.fr ❷ 09.30–23.00; 09.00–24.00 mid-June–Aug, Easter weekend & spring school holidays; last lift half-hour before closing Ⓝ Metro: Bir-Hakeim

Tour Montparnasse

Although it is a black blight on the Paris skyline, the Tour Montparnasse redeems itself through its spectacular view from the 56th floor. It has a 210-m (689-ft)-high terrace and café, the loftiest in Paris and the ideal place to drink in spectacular views. ❸ rue de l'Arrivée, 15th ❶ 01 45 38 52 56 Ⓦ www.tourmontparnasse56.com ❷ 09.30–23.30 (Apr–Sept); 09.30–22.30 Sun–Thur, 09.30–23.00 Fri & Sat (Oct–Mar); last lift half-hour before closing Ⓝ Metro: Montparnasse-Bienvenüe

CULTURE

Les Catacombes de Paris

The Catacombs came about when the Cimetière des Innocents became a threat to public health. All the bones were collected and

▲ *The Tour Eiffel stands tall above Paris*

transferred into this ossuary, which can still send a shiver up your vertebrae. ⓐ 1 av. du Colonel Henri Rol-Tanguy, 14th ⓣ 01 42 23 47 63 ⓦ www.catacombes-de-paris.fr ⓛ 10.00–16.00 Tues–Sun ⓝ Metro: Denfert-Rochereau

Fondation Cartier

The Fondation Cartier, established in 1984, is a private foundation for contemporary art. Huge windows let in the natural light, while outside grounds filled with tall trees emphasise the height of the display space and give a sense of bringing the outdoors in. Exhibitions focus on individual artists or themes from design to photography, painting to video. ⓐ 261 blvd Raspail, 14th ⓣ 01 42 18 56 50 ⓦ www.fondation.cartier.com ⓛ 11.00–20.00 Tues–Sun ⓝ Metro: Raspail or Denfert-Rochereau

Musée Delacroix

The painter's last home and atelier is now a charming, intimate museum, with displays of his work as well as memorabilia and letters to friends such as Charles Baudelaire and Georges Sand. Admission is free on the first Sunday of the month. ⓐ 6 rue de Furstenberg, 6th ⓣ 01 44 41 86 50 ⓦ www.musee-delacroix.fr ⓛ 09.30–17.00 Wed–Mon (until 17.30 Sat & Sun June–Aug) ⓝ Metro: Saint-Germain-des-Prés or Mabillon

Musée du Luxembourg

Some of the city's most important visiting exhibitions are held in the former orangery of the Senate building in the Jardin du Luxembourg. ⓐ 19 rue de Vaugirard, 6th ⓣ 01 42 34 25 95; reservations: 08 92 68 46 94 ⓦ www.museeduluxembourg.fr ⓛ 10.00–20.00 Sun–Thur, 10.00–22.00 Fri & Sat ⓝ RER B: Luxembourg

Musée Maillol Fondation Dina Vierny

This museum displays works by Maillol, including sculptures and paintings, as well as works from the private collection of Dina Vierny, such as those by Matisse, Gauguin, Rousseau and Kandinsky. It also holds temporary exhibitions of such well-known artists as Dufy and Fernando Botero. The charming, barrel-vaulted café in the basement serves drinks and snacks. ⓐ 59 rue de Grenelle, 7th ⓣ 01 42 22 59 58 ⓦ www.museemaillol.com ⓛ 10.30–19.00 Sat–Thur, 10.30–21.30 Fri ⓜ Metro: Rue du Bac

Musée du Montparnasse

Visiting this museum is like stepping back in time to 19th-century Paris. The entrance into this charming former painter's studio/canteen is via a peaceful cobbled alleyway. ⓐ 21 av. du Maine, 15th ⓣ 01 42 22 91 96 ⓦ www.museedumontparnasse.net ⓛ 12.30–19.00 Tues–Sun ⓜ Metro: Montparnasse-Bienvenüe

Musée d'Orsay

More than a museum, this grand structure, built as a train station for the World Fair in 1900, is an attraction in itself. The light-filled rooms and lofty, luminous central gallery set off some of the world's greatest artworks to their best advantage. The permanent collection encompasses the whole range of fine arts from the mid-19th century to the early 20th. The upper floor is devoted to Impressionists and Post-Impressionists, with famous works by Monet, Renoir, Degas, Cézanne, Pissarro, Sisley and Van Gogh. As well as the permanent collections, there are always rotating exhibitions. In summer, the open-air terrace on level five gives a fabulous view of the Seine and all the historic riverfront buildings. Admission to the museum is free on the first Sunday of the month.

⬤ *Visit the fabulous art collection in the cavernous Musée d'Orsay*

The Passerelle de Solférino pedestrian bridge across the Seine links the Musée d'Orsay in a graceful steel arch with the Jardin des Tuileries on the Right Bank. ❸ 62 rue de Lille, 7th ❶ 01 40 49 48 14 ❿ www.musee-orsay.fr ❶ 09.30–18.00 Tues, Wed & Fri–Sun, 09.30–21.45 Thur ❿ Metro: Solférino

Musée du Quai Branly

This museum along the Seine next to the Eiffel Tower houses arts and artefacts from the civilisations of Africa, Asia, Oceania and the Americas. Among its collections are items moved from the Musée de l'Homme and the Musée des Arts d'Afrique et d'Océanie. ❸ 55 quai Branly, 7th ❶ 01 56 61 70 00 ❿ www.quaibranly.fr ❶ 11.00–19.00 Tues, Wed & Sun, 11.00–21.00 Thur–Sat ❿ Metro: Iéna

Musée Rodin

The Musée Rodin provides a pleasant, green escape in the heart of Paris. Housed in a delightful 18th-century mansion, the museum contains bronze and marble work by Auguste Rodin (1840–1917), as well as works by Van Gogh, Monet, Renoir and others. Famous works such as *The Thinker*, *The Kiss* and *Eve* are scattered through the garden, which may be visited separately. ❸ 79 rue de Varenne, 7th ❶ 01 44 18 61 10 ❿ www.musee-rodin.fr ❶ 10.00–17.45 Tues–Sun (summer); 10.00–16.45 Tues–Sun (winter) ❿ Metro: Varenne

Musée Zadkine

The Russian artist Ossip Zadkine bequeathed his home and garden to the city of Paris. Some 100 of his works here include distinctive sculptures of bronze and tree trunks. ❸ 100 bis rue d'Assas, 6th ❶ 01 55 42 77 20 ❿ www.zadkine.paris.fr ❶ 10.00–18.00 Tues–Sun ❿ RER B: Port-Royal; metro: Notre-Dame-des-Champs or Vavin

Muséum National d'Histoire Naturelle

It's Jurassic Park without the violence at this natural history museum, where you can see reconstructions of dinosaurs, African game such as giraffes, and marine species. The evolution gallery, with its extinct and threatened section, makes you realise what we need to protect and preserve. **a** Jardin des Plantes, 36 rue Geoffroy Saint-Hilaire, 5th **t** 01 40 79 56 01 **w** www.mnhn.fr **l** 10.00–18.00 Wed–Mon **n** Metro: Jussieu

RETAIL THERAPY

La Bagagerie These stores sell all kinds of bags, from little clutches and practical office totes to wheeled suitcases. Prices are reasonable and staff friendly. Several locations, including **a** 41 rue du Four, 6th **t** 01 45 48 85 88 **w** www.labagagerie.com **l** 10.00–19.00 Mon–Sat **n** Metro: Mabillon

Le Bon Marché The oldest department store in Paris is nonetheless *très chic*, known for its ready-to-wear items, household goods and La Grande Epicerie (at No 38), with some 5,000 of the world's finest foodstuffs. Some of the little streets around Le Bon Marché, such as Rue de l'Abbé Grégoire and Rue Saint-Placide, often have sales and low prices. **a** 24 rue de Sèvres, 7th **t** 01 44 39 80 00 **w** www.lebonmarche.com **l** 10.00–20.00 Mon–Wed & Sat, 10.00–21.00 Thur & Fri **n** Metro: Sèvres-Babylone

Debauve et Gallais In 1800, Louis XVI's personal pharmacists founded this store, which is now a famous chocolatier. **a** 30 rue des Saints-Pères, 7th **t** 01 45 48 54 67 **w** www.debauve-et-gallais.com **l** 09.00–19.00 Mon–Sat **n** Metro: Saint-Germain-des-Prés or Sèvres-Babylone

Des Filles à la Vanille With three outlets on the Left Bank, Des Filles à la Vanille stocks clothes, accessories and bags for women. ⓐ 1 rue de l'Ancienne Comédie (corner of rue de Buci, off pl. Henri Mondor), 6th ⓣ 01 43 26 61 66 ⓦ www.desfillesalavanille.com ⓛ 11.00–19.30 ⓝ Metro: Odéon

La Maison Ivre This small boutique sells distinctive Provençal ceramics with jugs, bowls, tiles and other items coloured in the warm hues of the Mediterranean. ⓐ 38 rue Jacob, 6th ⓣ 01 42 60 01 85 ⓦ www.maison-ivre.com ⓛ 10.30–19.00 Mon–Sat ⓝ Metro: Saint-Germain-des-Prés

Zadig & Voltaire Designer clothes and bags by such creators as Helmut Lang and Yoshi Nagasawa. Several locations, including ⓐ 1 rue du Vieux-Colombier, 6th ⓣ 01 43 29 18 29 ⓦ www.zadig-et-voltaire.com ⓛ 10.30–19.30 Mon–Sat ⓝ Metro: Saint-Sulpice

TAKING A BREAK

La Coupole £ ❶ This famous 1900s brasserie in Montparnasse has rotating artwork displays, such as portraits of celebrated patrons of the past (like Hemingway and Jean-Paul Sartre). It is open for full meals, but for a light snack, the *Formule Thé* includes a tasty pastry, such as a seasonal fruit tart, and tea, delicious hot chocolate or coffee. ⓐ 102 blvd du Montparnasse, 6th ⓣ 01 43 20 14 20 ⓦ www.lacoupole-paris.com ⓛ 08.00–24.00 Mon–Wed, 08.00–01.00 Thur & Fri, 08.30–01.00 Sat, 08.30–24.00 Sun ⓝ Metro: Vavin

Les Deux Magots & Café de Flore £ ❷ & ❸ Since the late 19th/early 20th century, these two famous cafés on Boulevard Saint-Germain

have welcomed writers, artists and intellectuals, including Trotsky, Hemingway, Camus, Sartre and Simone de Beauvoir. Today, both sponsor writers' prizes to keep up the literary tradition.

Les Deux Magots has comfy wooden chairs, polished glass and brass, waiters in bow ties, black suits and long white aprons, and a view of the tower of the Saint-Germain-des-Prés church. English newspapers are available. ⓐ 6 pl. Saint-Germain-des-Prés, 6th ⓣ 01 45 48 55 25 ⓦ www.lesdeuxmagots.fr ⓛ 07.30–00.30 ⓝ Metro: Saint-Germain-des-Prés

Café de Flore is just as charming, and the hot chocolate here, served in a Flore-engraved silver jug, equals that of the neighbouring Deux Magots. ⓐ 172 blvd Saint-Germain, 6th ⓣ 01 45 48 55 26 ⓦ www.cafedeflore.fr ⓛ 07.00–02.00 ⓝ Metro: Saint-Germain-des-Prés

🔺 *Saint-Germain-des-Prés church tower*

Le Baba Bourgeois £–££ ❹ Enjoy a good brunch and a great view at this 1970s Italian-designed restaurant. ❸ 5 quai de la Tournelle, 5th ❶ 01 44 07 46 75 ❿ www.lebababourgeois.com ❶ 11.00–23.30 Tues–Sat; brunch: 11.30–17.00 Sun ❿ Metro: Pont Marie

Le Procope ££ ❺ Here in the oldest café in Paris (1686), Diderot and d'Alembert began compiling their encyclopaedia in 1727. Le Procope is known for its *cuisine traditionnelle*. ❸ 13 rue de l'Ancienne Comédie (off pl. Henri Mondor), 6th ❶ 01 40 46 79 00 ❿ www.procope.com ❶ 11.30–24.00 ❿ Metro: Odéon

AFTER DARK

RESTAURANTS
La Brasserie Saint Benoît £ ❻ Good traditional French fare, often with a complimentary kir, is served in this simple restaurant in the Saint-Germain district. ❸ 26 rue Saint-Benoît, 6th ❶ 01 45 48 29 66 ❿ http://ausaintbenoit.fr ❶ 12.00–23.30 Mon–Thur, 12.00–24.00 Fri–Sun ❿ Metro: Saint-Germain-des-Prés

Le Café du Commerce £ ❼ The historic café is spread over three levels around an atrium hung with cascading vines. With starters such as excellent *salade de chèvre chaud* (hot goat's cheese salad) and main courses such as grilled pork knuckle, steak with pepper sauce or fish, the Commerce is excellent value. ❸ 51 rue du Commerce, 15th ❶ 01 45 75 03 27 ❿ www.lecafeducommerce.com ❶ 12.00–15.00, 19.00–24.00 ❿ Metro: Avenue Émile Zola or Commerce

58 Tour Eiffel £–££ ❽ If prices in the Jules Verne (see page 116) are too stratospheric, 58 Tour Eiffel is more reasonably priced

and has a pretty view too. ⓐ Level One, Eiffel Tower, 7th ⓣ 08 25 56 66 62 ⓦ www.restaurants-toureiffel.com ⓝ Metro: Bir-Hakeim

Le Bouillon Racine £–££ ⑨ In this Art Nouveau-style restaurant you can enjoy good value, traditional meals. ⓐ 3 rue Racine, 6th ⓣ 01 44 32 15 60 ⓦ www.bouillon-racine.com ⓣ 12.00–01.00 (last orders 23.00). Note that at weekends there are two sittings, so book well in advance ⓝ Metro: Cluny La Sorbonne

Le Zyriab ££ ⑩ Known for its couscous and its fabulous view of Notre-Dame and the Seine, this Moroccan restaurant sits atop the Institut du Monde Arabe (see Multicultural Paris, pages 118–19). ⓐ 1 rue des Fossés-Saint-Bernard, 5th ⓣ 01 55 42 55 42 ⓦ www. imarabe.org ⓣ Lunch: 11.00–15.00; tea: 15.00–18.30; dinner: 19.30–23.30 Tues–Sun (closed Sun dinner) ⓝ Metro: Jussieu

Le Jules Verne £££ ⑪ For high-class, high-altitude (and high-priced) fare, try the Michelin-starred Le Jules Verne restaurant, located on the second level of the Eiffel Tower. The restaurant has its own lift and terrace. Diners have an excellent view of the city stretching along the river. ⓐ Level Two, Eiffel Tower, 7th ⓣ 01 45 55 61 44 ⓦ www.lejulesverne-paris.com ⓣ 12.15–13.30, 19.00–21.30 ⓝ Metro: Bir-Hakeim

BARS, CLUBS & ENTERTAINMENT

Le Bar du Marché This fashionable bar painted bright red on the corner of Buci and Rue de Seine is trendy by night and great for people-watching on sunny afternoons as a pavement café. Waiters wear overalls, the market vendors' dress code of yore. Ideal for a sunny breakfast *en terrasse*. ⓐ 75 rue de Seine, 6th ⓣ 01 43 26 55 15 ⓣ 08.00–02.00 ⓝ Metro: Mabillon

Bâteau Six-Huit A trendy dance club, theatre and concert venue on the banks of the Seine. ⓐ quai de Montebello, 5th ⓣ 06 60 47 38 52/ 01 46 34 53 05 ⓦ www.six-huit.com ⓛ Opening times vary according to event ⓝ Metro: Saint-Michel

Le Batofar Another buzzing and popular dance club on the Seine. ⓐ Opposite 11 quai François Mauriac, east of quai de la Tournelle ⓣ 09 71 25 50 61 ⓦ www.batofar.org ⓛ 19.00–04.00 Tues, 21.00–04.00 Wed–Sat ⓝ Metro: Quai de la Gare

Caveau de la Huchette Located in a basement cellar, this is a jazz institution in the heart of Saint-Michel. ⓐ 5 rue de la Huchette, 5th ⓣ 01 43 26 65 05 ⓦ www.caveaudelahuchette.fr ⓛ 21.30–02.30 Sun–Wed, 21.30–dawn Thur–Sat ⓝ Metro: Saint-Michel

Gare Montparnasse Watch a night-time phenomenon roll through the Left Bank every Friday night, when masses of rollerbladers take over the streets, leaving from the Gare Montparnasse in the 15th *arrondissement* at 22.00 (see page 33). ⓦ www.pari-roller.com ⓝ Metro: Montparnasse-Bienvenüe

La Mezzanine de l'Alcazar The Mezzanine bar of the Alcazar restaurant is lively with DJs or pop/rock singers, creating a great ambience for a drink or a dance. ⓐ 62 rue Mazarine, 6th ⓣ 01 53 10 19 99 ⓦ www.alcazar.fr ⓛ 19.00–01.00 Sun–Thur, 19.00–02.00 Fri & Sat ⓝ Metro: Odéon

NIGHT VIEWS
The **Musée National du Moyen Age** (ⓐ 6 pl. Paul-Painlevé, 5th ⓝ Metro: Cluny La Sorbonne) in the Hôtel de Cluny is impressive

MULTICULTURAL PARIS

Visitors to Paris can only benefit from the city's increasingly multi-ethnic make-up as new and varied influences broaden the cultural range of what it has to offer.

In the last 50 years or so, immigrants from France's former colonies in Algeria, Morocco and West Africa, as well as those from China, the Caribbean and Eastern Europe, have made Paris their home. This infusion of cultures has brought with it a whole new selection of intriguing museums and galleries, shops selling goods from around the world, and a fine collection of restaurants serving foreign cuisine.

Some *quartiers* have a varied mix: in the culturally diverse Belleville area in the north, there are Thai and Vietnamese restaurants, Turkish cafés, Arab grocery stores and kosher butchers. Ménilmontant, east of République, has couscous and tagine restaurants competing with Senegalese cuisine.

Generally, though, individual ethnic groups have settled in well-defined areas such as the predominantly North African Goutte d'Or in the 18th *arrondissement* and the Cambodian, Vietnamese, Laotian and Chinese sections of the 13th. The main Jewish community is based around Rue des Rosiers in the Marais, with its delicatessens and restaurants.

'Little India' in the 10th *arrondissement* started out in the 1970s as a couple of shops in a covered arcade, Passage Brady. Now, the area is full of curry restaurants, grocers and stores selling traditional Indian saris and incense.

The area around the Barbès-Rochechouart metro station is a West African and West Indian neighbourhood, and a great place to buy dazzling dresses or browse in food markets that sell tropical produce and exotic spices.

Arab culture is centred around the beautiful **Institut du Monde Arabe** (Institute of the Arab World ⓐ 1 rue des Fossés-Saint-Bernard, 5th ⓣ 01 40 51 38 38 ⓦ www.imarabe.org ⓛ 10.00–18.00 Tues–Sun; library: 13.00–20.00 Tues–Sat ⓜ Metro: Jussieu). The 1,600 exterior panels covering its south façade adjust automatically according to sunlight to create a peaceful, reflective atmosphere. Beside the museum's extensive displays of Arab culture, the Institut has a library, a shop, a tea salon serving the city's best mint tea, and a rooftop terrace and restaurant that has a superb view of the Seine and Notre-Dame.

Chinatown, near Place d'Italie metro station, is as much Southeast Asian as it is Chinese. Giant supermarkets such as Tangs Frères sell every conceivable delicacy of the East, including galangal, fish paste, dried lemongrass, chunks of tamarind, and fresh Chinese vegetables such as pak choi. Here, Chinese silk dresses and other Asian clothes are sold at discount prices.

If you don't have time to explore the whole city, a quicker way of getting a grip on Paris's multiple cultural faces is to visit the **Cité Nationale de l'Histoire de l'Immigration** (ⓐ Palais de la Porte Dorée, 293 av. Daumesnil, 12th ⓣ 01 53 59 58 60 ⓦ www.histoire-immigration.fr ⓛ 10.00–17.30 Tues–Fri, 10.00–19.00 Sat & Sun ⓜ Metro: Porte Dorée). This controversial recently opened museum tries to show the different impacts that migrants have had in France, through music, language, art and everyday objects.

enough by day on account of its medieval artefacts and tapestries, but when spotlit at night and viewed from Boulevard Saint-Michel this ancient building with its Gallo-Roman baths is an awesome, impressive sight in central Paris.

The Seine and its bridges and buildings illuminated at night are a majestic sight. It's one of the best experiences of Paris you will ever have, if the evening is fine. Stand on the Pont Royal or the Pont du Carrousel, near the Louvre, and look back to the splendid sight of Notre-Dame, also illuminated at night. Buskers come out as dusk falls, and beneath you on the river all kinds of boats will be passing, including the brightly lit dinner boats.

These dinner boats also provide a wonderful view of Paris at night, with unfamiliar views of familiar buildings. In addition, they do also provide a better meal than you might expect from such a popular tourist attraction.

Spending a night in Montmartre is to have a very Parisian experience, and find time to go to Sacré-Coeur for the night-time view over the city, across to the Eiffel Tower.

The Eiffel Tower naturally steals the skyline show each night, when it is bathed in gold and sparkling. For the best views go to the Trocadéro and look across the river. It's a lively place with vendors and buskers adding to the fun, and you'll certainly want to try to capture the view of the night-time Eiffel Tower on your camera. Take a tripod if you have one, though there are walls to set the camera on too. The views from the top of the Tour Montparnasse are also exquisite on a clear night and well worth the lift ride to the top (see page 106).

▶ *Medieval masterpiece: the Cathédrale Notre-Dame at Reims*

 # OUT OF TOWN
trips

Auvers-sur-Oise

For fans of Vincent van Gogh, a visit to the village of Auvers-sur-Oise is a pilgrimage. The artist lived his last two months here, painting some of his most famous works. He took such solace in Auvers that he painted prolifically, producing 78 works during his brief visit. This delightful village – some 30 km (18½ miles) northwest of Paris – with its stone houses, pretty gardens and cobbled streets remains much as it was in the artist's day, and is still a vibrant artists' community with a number of galleries. The masterpieces painted by Van Gogh and others are indicated throughout by signs called La Mémoire des Lieux, where copies of the paintings are shown at the locations of the scenes painted.

The **Auvers Tourist Office** has brochures, including those of self-guided walks, with maps marking the famous attractions and settings of Van Gogh's works. ❸ Manoir des Colombières, rue de la Sansonne ❶ 01 30 36 10 06 ❿ www.auvers-sur-oise.com ⏰ 09.30–12.30, 14.00–18.00 (closes 17.00 in winter)

GETTING THERE

Take the SNCF train from Gare du Nord or Gare Saint-Lazare to Pontoise and change for Auvers-sur-Oise (direction Creil). Trains are frequent (every 20–30 minutes) with a total journey time of one hour. From April to November there are usually direct services on Saturdays, Sundays and public holidays.

If you're driving, take the A15 in the direction of Cergy-Pontoise, leave the motorway at exit 7 and take the RN 184 (direction Beauvais) as far as Méry-sur-Oise, then follow the signs for Auvers-sur-Oise.

Auvers-sur-Oise

RUE DES TOURNELLES

Galerie d'Art Contemporain

RUE DU MONCEL

RUE DE RAJON

RUE DE PARIS

RUE EMILE BERNARD

RUE FERDINAND MESNY

Église d'Auvers

1

RUE DE L'ÉGLISE

AVENUE MARCEL PERRIN

RUE MARCEL MARTIN

CHEMIN DE PILAGE

Oise

S DES CALPONS

CHEMIN DES VALLÉES À BURY

RUE DU FORT DE VAUX

RUE MONTAUBE

RUE DE FER SAINT-VINCENT

CHEMIN DE PILAGE

Atelier de Daubigny

Auberge Ravoux/ Maison de Van Gogh

3

RUE DAUBIGNY

RUE DU GÉNÉRAL DE GAULLE

Musée Daubigny

2

PLACE DE LA MAIRIE

RUE DU POIS

RAVINE DES PONCEAUX

SENTIER DE LA RAVINE PONCEAUX

Musée de l'Absinthe

RUE DES VERTS

RUE DES PONCEAUX

R ALPHONSE CALLE

RUE DE LA BOURGOGNE

RAVINE DES VALLÉES

Château d'Auvers

2

RUE DE ZUNDERT

RUE DU CLOS

RUE EUGÈNE FALQUERT

RUE VAN GOGH

RUE DE LA BOURGOGNE

ALLÉE LÉONIDE BOURGES

RUE DU PARC

RUE DES FLEURS

RUE CARNOT

RUE FRÉDÉRIC

RUE FRANÇOIS MITTERRAND

RUE DU RÉSERVOIR

RUE BOUCHER

RUE ÉMILE BOGGIO

RUE EUG

Maison du Dr Gachet

CHEMIN DE LA LONGUE RUE

SENTIER DES CHAMPS

RUE DU DOCTEUR GACHET

RUE FRANÇOIS VILLON

4

RUE LOUIS GANNE

RUE ROGER TAGLIANA

RUE DES AUNAIES

N

0   250 metres
0   250 yards

SIGHTS & ATTRACTIONS

Château d'Auvers

An excellent introduction to the Impressionist period in Auvers is the Château d'Auvers's audiovisual romp through the world of such artists as Daubigny, Pissarro, Cézanne and Renoir. ⓐ rue de Léry ⓣ 01 34 48 48 45 ⓦ www.chateau-auvers.fr ⓛ 10.30–18.00 Tues–Sun (closes 16.30 in winter)

Église d'Auvers

Perhaps the most poignant sight for many visitors is the church here. The delightful painting of it, *L'Église d'Auvers*, framed by a vibrant blue sky, now hangs in the Musée d'Orsay in Paris (see pages 109–11). The Romano-Gothic church is topped by a bell tower. ⓐ rue de l'Église ⓛ 09.00–18.00

Maison de Van Gogh

Van Gogh lived his final days in a tiny attic room in the Auberge Ravoux, also called the Maison de Van Gogh. The room, sparse and emotive, with a tiny skylight, has been preserved as it was when Van Gogh died. One gets a sense of the despair that the artist felt towards the end, evident in such paintings as *Wheatfield with Crows*. Yet he produced many cheerful and vibrant works, such as the *Escalier d'Auvers*, a delightful scene of a staircase at the top of Rue de la Sansonne.

Van Gogh produced many other famous and important works in Auvers, such as his self-portrait and the *Portrait of Dr Gachet*, which now hang in the Musée d'Orsay. The Van Gogh Institute is determined to return his Auvers canvases to the room where he lived. ⓐ pl. de la Mairie ⓣ 01 30 36 60 60 ⓦ www.maisondevangogh.fr ⓛ 10.00–18.00 Wed–Sun Mar–Oct

Musée de l'Absinthe (Absinthe Museum)

A heady influence on many artists, including Van Gogh, was absinthe, a potent aperitif that preceded today's aniseed drink. The cloudy green beverage could be ruinous, as many lithographs and posters in this excellent museum show. ➋ 44 rue Alphonse Calle ➊ 01 30 36 83 26 ➌ 13.30–18.00 Wed–Fri, 11.00–18.00 Sat & Sun (Apr–Oct); 11.00–18.00 Sat & Sun (Nov–Mar)

▲ *The majestic Château d'Auvers*

AUVERS'S OTHER FAMOUS ARTIST

Although Auvers will always be synonymous with Van Gogh, the village was also the adopted home of another significant 19th-century painter, Charles-François Daubigny. Daubigny found fame as an alumnus of the 'Barbizon school', whose members focused on the subject of nature; thus it was that he came to Auvers to paint the River Oise. The surrounding areas also inspired him, and while he lived here he produced works such as *Auvers-sur-Oise* (1868), works that subsequently influenced the Impressionists.

Though in no sense a posthumous superstar like Van Gogh, Daubigny achieved far more recognition in his lifetime than Vincent did in his. He was made an Officer of the Legion of Honour, one of France's highest honours, and died in Paris in 1878. The Atelier de Daubigny is a museum dedicated to his life and work.

Atelier de Daubigny ⓐ 61 rue Daubigny ⓣ 01 34 48 03 03 ⓦ www.atelier-daubigny.com ⓛ 14.00–18.30 Thur–Sun (Apr–Sept)

RETAIL THERAPY

Auvers Tourist Office Lots of art books and postcards, and trinkets, such as painters'-palette earrings. Contact details on page 122.

Un Certain Regard Art and craftwork gallery with art books and original works by 13 local artists. Friendly, original and agreeable, even if you don't buy anything. ⓐ 2 rue Montmaur ⓣ 06 71 17 06 13 ⓛ 10.30–12.30, 15.00–19.30 Thur–Sun

Galerie d'Art Contemporain This contemporary art gallery holds exhibitions of artists' work and sells reproductions of Van Gogh works as well as original works of contemporary amateur artists.
ⓐ 5 rue du Montcel ⓣ 01 34 48 00 10 ⓛ 14.00–16.00 Tues–Sun

TAKING A BREAK

Le Chemin des Peintres £ ❶ Located in an 1848 building, this charming restaurant-tea salon serves both traditional and modern cuisine made from local farm produce. ⓐ 3 bis rue de Paris ⓣ 01 30 36 14 15 ⓦ www.le-chemin-des-peintres.fr ⓛ Lunch: Wed–Sun; dinner: Sat; tea salon: 11.00–17.00 Mon–Fri; events: Fri evening (times vary)

La Guinguette £ ❷ La Guinguette is one of three eating choices at the Château itself, with tables both outside, on a terrace, and inside, in a lovely 17th-century hall. You can elect just to have a drink if you wish, or can enjoy the good-value fixed-price set lunch. ⓐ Château d'Auvers, rue de Léry ⓣ 01 34 48 48 45 ⓦ www.chateau-auvers.fr ⓛ 12.00–14.30 Tues–Sun

Auberge Ravoux £–££ ❸ An artists' café since 1876, this cosy restaurant in the Maison de Van Gogh serves such treats as Gigot de Sept Heures (leg of lamb cooked for seven hours), the house speciality. ⓐ 8 rue de la Sansonne ⓣ 01 30 36 60 60 ⓛ Lunch: 12.00–16.00; tea salon: 10.00–12.00, 16.00–18.00 (Mar–Oct only)

La Ferme du Périgord ££ ❹ In winter, gorge on hearty southwest cuisine; in summer, enjoy the *terrasse*. Booking advised. ⓐ 5 rue Marceau ⓣ 01 34 48 06 42 ⓦ www.lafermeduperigord.com/ferme-perigord.swf ⓛ 12.15–14.00, 19.15–21.00 Tues & Thur–Sat, 12.15–14.00 Sun

Reims

Reims (pronounced 'Rhants'), 143 km (89 miles) northeast of Paris in the heart of champagne country, is a magnet for lovers of the bubbly stuff.

This area is also known for its tumultuous history, gentle countryside and one of Europe's finest Gothic cathedrals. The 'Coronation Capital of France' is a city of ancient abbeys and modern factories, art museums, cobbled squares and modern, red-brick areas. Set among the extensive hills of vineyards, atop some 250 km (155 miles) of chalk caves storing millions of bottles of ageing effervescent wine, Reims is an attractive city well worth at least a day trip from Paris. In addition to its magnificent cathedral and, some would say, even more magnificent champagne houses, Reims has much more for the visitor to enjoy. Its oldest Roman structure is the Mars Gate, thought to date from the 3rd or 4th century AD. Building on the Palace of Tau, the Archbishop's Palace, began in 1498, and today it is open to the public as a museum.

Europe's northernmost grape-growing area is a pleasant train ride from the French capital. The first sign of champagne country comes just outside the town of Epernay, where the grand buildings of some venerable champagne houses, like ornate railway stations, are seen to the right. Soon after come vineyards planted with orderly rows of grapes.

Day tickets for buses within Reims are €3.20 and include the airport shuttle. With these, it is easy to get around to some of the champagne houses a few blocks from the city centre, although it is also possible to walk to some with a map from the tourist board.

Comité Régional du Tourisme

ⓦ www.tourisme-champagne-ardenne.com

Reims

0	250 metres
0	250 yards

	POI
↑	Cathedral
i	Information
⊡	Railway Stn

N

RUE M. FOURNAUX

AVENUE DE LAON

RUE PRÉSIDENT F.D. ROOSEVELT

RUE GOSSET

Musée de la Reddition

RUE ÉDOUARD MIGNOT

BOULEVARD JULES CÉSAR

RUE DU CHAMP DE MARS

RUE DU DOCTEUR LEMOINE

Monument Aux Morts

RUE DU CHAMP DE MARS

RUE DE LA JUSTICE

PLACE DE LA RÉPUBLIQUE

RUE COQLIEBERT

BOULEVARD JOFFRE

BOULEVARD FOCH

Marché Couvert des Halles

BOULEVARD LUNDY

RUE CAMILLE LENOIR

Basses Promenades

RUE DU GAL SARRAIL

RUE DE MARS

RUE DU TEMPLE

RUE LINGUET

BOULEVARD GÉNÉRAL LECLERC

RUE THIERS

Hôtel de Ville

RUE J. ROUSSEAU

AVENUE JEAN JAURÈS

COURS J.B. LANGLET

Musée Le Vergeur

RUE COURMEAUX

PLACE ARISTIDE BRIAND

RUE DE CERNAY

RUE DE L'ÉTAPE

RUE DES ÉLUS

PLACE DU FORUM

RUE CÉRÈS

DE BRIMONT

Pl. DROUET D'ERLON

RUE DE TELLIERS

RUE BURETTE

RUE CONDORCET

PLACE MYRON HERRICH

RUE E DESTEUQUE

i

RUE DES POISSONNIERS

RUE JEANNE D'ARC

RUE DE VESLE

Palais de Justice

PLACE DU CARDINAL LUÇON

Cathédrale ↑ Notre-Dame

RUE PONSARDIN

PLACE PAUL JAMOT

RUE HOUZEAU MUIRON

RUE MOISSONS

Musée des Beaux-Arts

Palais du Tau

RUE VOLTAIRE

BOULEVARD LA PAIX

RUE M. STUART

RUE CHANZY

RUE DE L'UNIVERSITÉ

BOULEVARD SAINT-MARCEAUX

RUE CHAMOL

RUE HINCMAR

PLACE DES LOGES COQUAULT

RUE DES

RUE DU BOULARD

RUE MAROT

RUE GERBERT

BD GEORGES CLEMENCEAU

RUE DES CAPUCINS

RUE DU JARD

BD PASTEUR

RUE PONSARDIN

BOULEVARD PAUL DOUMER

La Vesle

RUE DE VENISE

RUE DU BARBATRE

RUE CLOVIS

RUE DES CAPUCINS

RUE CARNETTA

AUTOROUTE

RUE DES CARMES

BOULEVARD VICTOR HUGO

Piper-Heidsieck

CHAUSSÉE BOCQUAINE

AV PAUL MARCHANDEAU

BOULEVARD DOCTEUR HENRI HENROT

RUE DES MOULINS

Planetarium

Musée de l'Anc Collège des Jésuites

BOULEVARD HENRY VASNIER

RUE CHAUSSÉE ST MARTIN

RUE DES MA RAI

RUE DU RUISSELET

RUE ARMONVILLE

PLACE SAINT-NICAISE

Taittinger

PLACE DU GÉNÉRAL GOURAND

Musée St-Rémi

RUE DU GRAND CERF

RUE A PETIT

Pommery

RUE CLOVIS CHÉZEL

PLACE DES DROITS DE L'HOMME

BVD DIANCOURT

Veuve Clicquot

Reims Tourist Board ❸ 2 rue Guillaume de Machault (beside the cathedral) ❶ 03 26 77 45 00 Ⓦ www.reims-tourisme.com ❶ 09.00–18.00 Mon–Sat (also booth at Christmas market daily in Dec)

🔺 *Cathédrale Notre-Dame up close and personal*

REIMS'S CROWNING GLORY

The Cathédrale Notre-Dame, which is every bit the equal of its Parisian namesake, is of great interest both historically and architecturally. UNESCO has gone so far as to call it 'one of the masterpieces of Gothic art', and it is certainly rich in ornamentation, with some 2,300 statues decorating the exterior. The interior has high arches and vaults with magnificent stained-glass windows at each end. At the south end, modern windows by Marc Chagall depict biblical scenes. The rose windows at the north end are even more impressive and ornate.

To any French people who still consider themselves monarchists, the cathedral has enormous resonance: starting with Clovis in 496, the country's monarchs were crowned on this site (the present structure was started in 1211 but was preceded by at least one other building). The coronation of Charles VII here in 1429 is particularly interesting as we know that Joan of Arc was present. Indeed, Charles was a key figure in the 17-year-old's campaign to rid this part of France of British and Burgundian domination. ☏ 08 92 30 17 51 🕐 07.30–19.30, free entrance, with (paying) guided visits in English and a visit to the towers

GETTING THERE

Trains for the one-and-three-quarter-hour trip to Reims depart from Paris several times a day from Gare de l'Est, so it is possible to leave in the morning, visit the city and several caves or vineyards, and be back in Paris by late evening, especially now thanks to the

TGV (45 minutes). Costs vary depending on the time of day and week. For details, visit ⓦ www.voyages-sncf.com

By car from Paris to Reims is 144 km (90 miles), around one and a half hours, via the A4.

SIGHTS & ATTRACTIONS

If a pleasant stroll is what you're after, then from the train station, Place Drouet d'Erlon, a charming pedestrian street lined with hotels, bars, several Irish pubs and shops leads into the city centre. A number of Roman remnants are on show right in the city, namely the Porte de Mars, enormous Roman arches dating from the year 200, and Place du Forum, a long semi-underground Roman gallery.

Cellar tours

Reims was built on bubbles and its major attraction remains champagne. The best way to appreciate it is through a tour of the cellars – but remember to dress warmly! More than a dozen of the famous houses offer tours, with rates ranging from €10 to €26. These are a bargain, as the price usually includes one or two glasses of champagne, which cost €8–10 each at local bars.

Guides lead tours deep into the chalk cellars, 15–25 m (49–82 ft) underground. These Roman quarries, abandoned since the 3rd century BC, were excavated to get stone for building. The subterranean labyrinths of cool caves were only later used for champagne-making and storage. Down in the dimly lit caverns stand row upon row of dusty champagne bottles going through the second fermentation.

Guides explain, step by step, the complex process of producing a bottle of bubbly, from picking to fermenting to blending, the second fermentation, *remuage* (turning the bottles to collect the sediment) and *dégorgement* (removing the sediment). They impart a real sense of the pride the great houses take in producing their fine champagnes.

Tours end in the tasting room, with a glass or two of the house's fine champagne to sample. There, oenologists may explain that the effervescent beverage is best sipped from tall tulip or flute glasses, which focus the tiny, perfect bubbles in continuous streams, rather than broad, fishbowl glasses, which dissipate bubbles and aroma.

Taittinger (ⓐ 9 pl. St-Nicaise ⓣ 03 26 85 84 33 ⓦ www.taittinger.fr ⓛ 09.30–11.50, 14.00–16.50 (mid-Mar–mid-Nov); 09.30–11.50, 14.00–16.20 Mon–Sat (mid-Nov–mid-Mar)), a relatively young house but with ancient cellars, provides one of the best tours. It starts with a short film in a screening room with large murals explaining the wine-making process. An extensive, one-hour tour with knowledgeable guides follows. The cellars have some ancient abbey doors and a statue of St John the Baptist, the patron saint of cellar workers.

Nearby, the **Pommery** house (ⓐ 5 pl. du Général Gourand ⓣ 03 26 61 62 55 ⓦ www.pommery.com ⓛ 09.30–19.00 Apr–mid-Nov; 10.00–18.00 mid-Nov–Mar ⓘ Booking required) is in the most impressive building, like a castle. Its traditional tour through part of its 18 km (11 miles) of cellars ends in a huge tasting room featuring an enormous carved barrel end and lots of other massive barrels.

Another good bet is the prestigious **Veuve Clicquot** house (ⓐ 1 pl. des Droits de l'Homme ⓣ 03 26 89 53 90 ⓦ www.veuve-clicquot.com ⓛ Mon–Sat (Apr–Oct); Mon–Fri (Nov–mid-Dec & mid-Jan–Mar) ⓘ Booking required) with its dimly lit *crayères* (chalk champagne cellars) and two centuries of fascinating history.

Details on all champagne houses can be found at ⓦ www.umc.fr. The tourist office has information on all champagne tours and the addresses of the cellars. Some tours are by appointment only or for

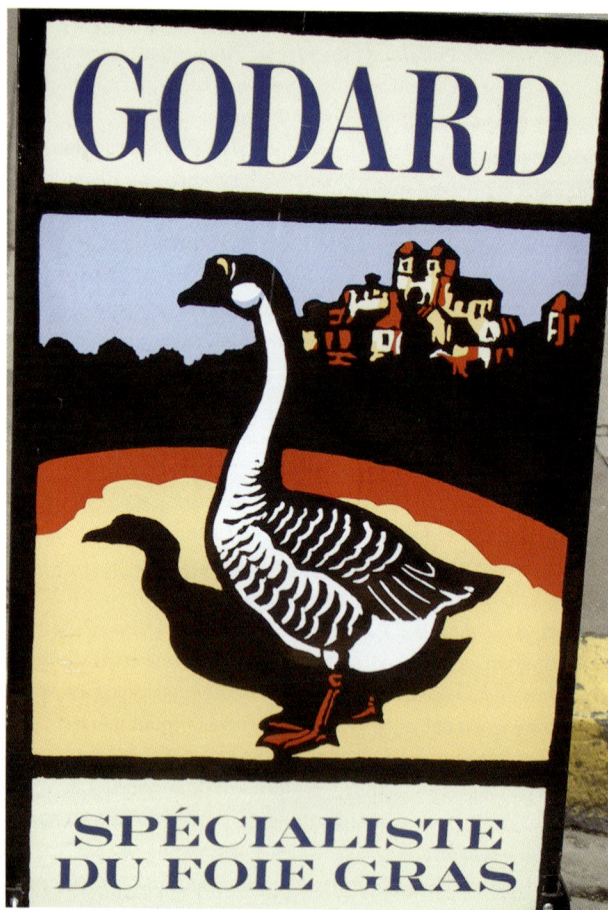

Local produce in Reims

groups. Others, such as Taittinger, have regular tours and it is just a matter of showing up. In most cases, it's usually best to call in advance.

Hot-air ballooning

If you want to get really high on the champagne region, take a hot-air balloon ride. Inflated balloons carrying four or five passengers lift gently away, over the slopes where grapes grow in patterned fields, the rows as orderly as bottles in the long cellars. The trip ends, appropriately enough, with ground crew waiting with fluted glasses, silver ice buckets and bottles of chilled *grand cru*. **Les Montgolfières Champenoises** (☎ 06 64 97 32 61 Ⓦ www.les-montgolfieres-champenoises.com) offers flights at dawn or two hours before sunset between mid-April and October; for advice on other companies in the area contact the tourist office. Flights usually cost around €190 per person.

Vineyard tours

Outside of the cellars, there are above-ground tours of the earlier part of the process – the growing and harvesting of grapes from Reims. Minibuses follow the official Route du Champagne tourist trail through the vineyards and past ancient villages. Some go to the quaint village of Hautvillers, and the old abbey of Hautvillers where the original Dom Perignon lived. Dom Perignon was born in 1638 and was cellar-master at the abbey when the wine produced here was mainly red. Despite what the locals may insist, he did not invent sparkling wine, which already existed and was probably first made in England. Dom Perignon simply worked on ways of preventing secondary fermentation in the bottles, which caused them to explode occasionally. Part of the abbey, greatly damaged during the French Revolution, is now a champagne museum. Various

tableaux depict how the innovative monk first stopped the bottles with cork (an idea from Spanish monks) and how he gave them their distinctive, long-necked shape.

A typical vineyard tour for groups of two to eight people, in a minibus, is €20 per person. They depart from Epernay Tourist Office at 09.30 or 14.30 according to the season. You can also choose a guided tour by foot or bike (€10 including bike rental). **Le Champagne Domi Moreau** ⓐ 11 rue du Bas, 51530 Mancy ⓣ 03 26 59 45 85 ⓦ www.champagne-domimoreau.com ⓛ Thur–Tues; call before visiting to check opening times

RETAIL THERAPY

Souvenir shops in the tourist information office and local stores sell boxes of traditional St Rémi Galettes (cookies), sandstone gargoyle replicas of the ones on the cathedral and other sandstone carvings of vineyard workers. All the champagne houses have shops.

Cave des Sacres Right near the cathedral, this has a wide range of souvenirs. This is a great place for champagne paraphernalia, such as elegant glass flutes with holders and silver-plated ice buckets. You can also buy local products like jars of mustard and local vinegars. ⓐ 7 pl. du Cardinal Luçon ⓣ 03 26 47 35 89 ⓦ www.cavedessacres.com ⓛ 09.30–19.00

La Grande Boutique du Vin Friendly and very competent staff go out of their way to find a wine, champagne or whisky to suit your taste (and budget). ⓐ 3 pl. Léon Bourgeois ⓣ 03 26 40 12 12 ⓦ www.vinscph.com ⓛ 09.00–12.30, 14.00–19.00 Mon–Fri, 09.00–19.30 Sat

⬛ *A vineyard just outside Epernay*

TAKING A BREAK

Café du Palais £ ❶ While this atmospheric café may be popular with tourists, by far the greatest number of clientele is local. Very good, friendly service accompanies the excellent wine list and fine family food (mum cooks the main courses, daughter the sweets, and the son manages the front). ❷ 14 pl. Myron-Herrich ❶ 03 26 47 52 54 Ⓦ www.cafedupalais.fr Ⓛ 10.00–21.30 Tues–Fri, dinner (until 23.00) Sat

Chez Anita £ ❷ Despite the name, Chez Anita serves up tasty Italian cuisine, with a long list of pasta dishes, risottos and home-made pizzas, though you will also find French delicacies such as escargots and foie gras too. ❷ 37 rue Ernest Renan ❶ 03 26 40 16 20 Ⓦ www. chez-anita.com Ⓛ 12.00–14.00, 19.00–22.00 (until 22.30 Sat & Sun)

Le Grand Café £ ❸ With its wood and mirrors, paintings and old black-and-white photographs of France, this café is a visual treat. The speciality of the house is *moules frites* (mussels with chips), served non-stop, and champagne. ❷ 92 pl. Drouet d'Erlon ❶ 03 26 47 61 50 Ⓦ www.le-grandcafe.com Ⓛ 11.30–24.00

Version Originale ££ ❹ Candlelit dinners are something special in this restaurant with its white décor and atmosphere of purity. The chef draws inspiration from around the world to create a frequently changing menu, and prices offer good value. ❷ 25 bis rue du Temple ❶ 03 26 02 69 32 Ⓦ www.vo-reims.fr Ⓛ 12.00–14.00, 19.00–22.00 Tues–Sat (until 22.30 Fri & Sat)

❶ *Follow the signs*

PRACTICAL
information

Directory

GETTING THERE

By air

Paris is easy to get to from pretty much anywhere in the world, with most major airlines offering flights from major international gateways. Low-cost airlines such as easyJet and Ryanair also fly to Paris from several small UK airports. Most flights come in at Roissy-Charles de Gaulle and Orly airports, with Beauvais specialising in charter and low-cost flights. See pages 48–9 for airport and transfer information.

⬥ *Terminal 2E at Roissy-Charles de Gaulle*

Airlines with direct flights to Paris include:

Air Canada Ⓦ www.aircanada.com

Air France Ⓦ www.airfrance.com

American Airlines Ⓦ www.aa.com

British Airways Ⓦ www.ba.com

Delta Airlines Ⓦ www.delta.com

easyJet Ⓦ www.easyjet.com

KLM Ⓦ www.klm.com

Ryanair Ⓦ www.ryanair.com

United Ⓦ www.united.com

US Airways Ⓦ www.usairways.com

Many people are aware that air travel emits CO_2, which contributes to climate change. You may be interested in the possibility of lessening the environmental impact of your flight through the charity **Climate Care** (Ⓦ www.climatecare.org), which offsets your CO_2 by funding environmental projects around the world.

By rail

The Eurostar provides fast, seamless connections from London's St Pancras International station to central Paris (Gare du Nord) in less than two and a half hours. By booking two months or more in advance, you can get great savings, and travel mid-week is cheaper than on weekends. Ⓦ www.eurostar.com

The Thalys high-speed train links Paris to Brussels and Amsterdam. Ⓦ www.thalys.com

For information and tickets for all rail travel (including high-speed trains called TGV) in France and Europe, contact the SNCF or visit one of their offices in Paris. ☎ 08 92 35 35 35 Ⓦ www.voyages-sncf.com

By road

Travelling by car from Calais to Paris, the 289 km (179 miles) takes just under three hours. Take the N1 south. Depending on where you approach Paris from, you'll join the ring road at one of the 30 *portes* (gateways) that punctuate the 35 km (22 miles) of expressway. Based on the area you are heading towards, you have a choice between the *périphérique intérieur* (inner ring road), which runs in a clockwise direction, and the *périphérique extérieur* (outer ring road), which runs counter-clockwise.

Traffic flow and journey times between gateways are displayed on illuminated overhead panels. Exit signs for each gateway into the city are given plenty of time in advance, so you can make sure you get in the right-hand lane. The speed limit is 80 km/h (50 mph) on ring roads and 50 km/h (31 mph) in urban areas. Driving is on the right and seat belts are mandatory, in the back too.

Travelling by coach is a good option for those on a budget who don't mind a little discomfort. **Eurolines** (Ⓦ www.eurolines.com) coaches operate year-round between London and Paris. The journey takes about 8–10 hours, with overnight services available. The Paris bus station is northeast of the city centre at Gallieni, with a metro station right next door. **Busabout** (Ⓦ www.busabout.com) has a 'hop-on, hop-off' option suitable for those who wish to travel around the whole of Europe, including Paris. There are coach links from Paris to all major mainland European cities.

By water

There are many connections from Britain to France by sea. For information on the main ferry services, see Ⓦ www.directferries.co.uk, Ⓦ www.condorferries.co.uk, Ⓦ www.aferry.co.uk, Ⓦ www.brittany-ferries.co.uk

ENTRY FORMALITIES

Citizens of EU countries require a passport or, if applicable, an identity card in order to enter France. Citizens of Australia, Canada, Finland, New Zealand, Norway, Sweden and the US need a passport but can stay for up to 90 days without a visa. South Africans need a tourist visa. Contact the Consulat Général de France in Johannesburg (📧 PO Box 1027 Parklands 2101) or Visa Services (📧 191 Jan Smuts Av., 3rd floor, Standard Bank Building, Rosebank 2196 ☎ (27) 11 778 56 02 🌐 www.consulfrance-jhb.org). All other passport holders should check with their nearest French embassy or consulate. For more information, see 🌐 www.diplomatie.gouv.fr

Visitors may bring in personal possessions and goods for personal use. The Single European Market allows visitors to bring in and take out most things as long as taxes have been paid on them in an EU country and they are for personal consumption. For more information, contact 🌐 www.douane.gouv.fr

MONEY

The euro is the currency of France and many other countries in the EU. €1 is divided into 100 cents. Notes come in €5, €10, €20, €50, €100, €200 and €500. Coins come in €1 and €2 and in 1, 2, 5, 10, 20 and 50 cents.

Bureaux de change, available at train stations, airports and main bank branches, are usually open late. Check exchange rates and commission charged before using any service. If you have an international credit or debit card, automatic teller machines (ATMs) are widely available and most have service in English. By far the majority of travellers today use ATMs, the most economical system. Credit cards are widely accepted, particularly Visa and MasterCard.

Make a note of your credit card company's 24-hour number in case your card is lost or stolen.

HEALTH, SAFETY & CRIME

There are no special food and drink precautions to take. Tap water is drinkable, unless otherwise marked. France is famous for its excellent healthcare, and the European Health Insurance Card entitles citizens from EU countries to the state-funded healthcare scheme in France or other EU countries in which they are staying. See the travel section of Ⓦ www.dh.gov.uk. For non-EU travellers, however, it can be expensive, so you should purchase your own health insurance before travelling.

In a medical emergency, call SAMU, the emergency ambulance service (Ⓣ 15). Firemen (*pompiers*) provide first aid and are usually first to the scene of an accident (Ⓣ 18). They can also help with other emergency situations. Medicines are available at pharmacies (indicated by a green cross), some of which are open on Sundays. Pharmacy staff are able to advise on all common ailments. For more serious health problems, ask your hotel to locate a doctor who is *conventionné* (state registered).

Violent crime is rare in the city centre and around the major tourist sights, although some of the *banlieues* (suburbs) are not safe after dark. However, pickpocketing is widespread, especially on the metro and other public transport, at major tourist sites and even in museums, so keep your bags and wallets closed and well out of reach, and be vigilant. Backpacks, particularly their front-zippered pockets, are a common target for pickpockets, so don't keep anything valuable in those, unless you carry them in front of you.

Pedestrians should be extremely careful when crossing the road; watch out for cars, motorbikes, scooters and even rollerbladers, as the average Parisian tends to take liberties where road safety is concerned. Look both ways before crossing, and make sure you respect the zebra crossings and traffic lights, as some drivers won't. Parisians of all ages seem to enjoy the thrill of dashing across at the last second; you may not want to do the same.

Hostess bars, particularly in the Pigalle neighbourhood, can charge exorbitant prices, so beware.

If you do require assistance, police are fairly obvious in dark-blue uniforms with the word 'police' prominently displayed. They are quite helpful, although most do not speak much English.

OPENING HOURS

Most services, shops and businesses are open all day from 09.00 or 09.30 to 19.00 or 20.00. Major department stores usually stay open late one night per week. Smaller boutiques often open later in the mornings, at around 10.00 or 11.00. On Sunday, most shops and businesses are closed, although Sunday shopping is prevalent in the Marais district and around the quays of Canal Saint-Martin.

Banking hours are usually 09.00–16.30 on weekdays, though some banks are open on Saturday.

Most museums are closed either Monday or Tuesday, but the larger ones have at least one night per week when they'll stay open until around 22.00. Note that last entry to museums is usually half an hour or an hour before closing, and that almost all museums are closed on public holidays.

TOILETS

Despite its poor reputation for public toilets, Paris does have some decent public facilities in parks, gardens and other public spaces. Most are supervised and charge a small fee for entry, but several 'superloos' (silver cubicles which look a little like spaceships) are available for free and are automatically cleaned after each visitor. Café owners do not usually welcome people using their toilets

unless they are paying customers, and some cafés even have coin-entry toilets. If caught short, pop into a department store, which usually offers free toilets; facilities in shopping centres and arcades are not always free of charge. Toilets in railway stations also charge a fee.

CHILDREN

Paris is generally child-friendly, with children welcome in most restaurants (although not as much as dogs!). Getting around by metro can be tiring for young children, however, as there are a lot of steps and long walks in the stations. This can also be hard for parents with buggies. Baby food, nappies and other necessities are available in supermarkets throughout the city. A full list of attractions and activities especially suitable for children can be found at ⓦ www.parisinfo.com

Disneyland Resort Paris (ⓣ 01 60 30 60 53/08 25 30 60 30 ⓦ www.disneylandparis.com ⓒ Check website as hours change seasonally, and park opens early for residents of resort hotel) is probably the biggest attraction for most kids. It is easily accessible by RER A east to Marne-la-Vallée-Chessy.

If you want your kids to learn while they play, book a session at the Cité des Enfants within the Cité des Sciences science and technology museum (see pages 88–9) at La Villette. During the one-and-a-half-hour time slot, youngsters aged 3 to 12 can engage in a host of fun interactive learning activities. Older children will enjoy the museum itself, since most exhibits and experiments are explained in English as well as French. Another interactive science museum is the **Palais de la Découverte** (ⓐ av. Franklin D Roosevelt, 8th ⓣ 01 56 43 20 21 ⓦ www.palais-decouverte.fr ⓒ 09.30–18.00 Tues–Sat, 10.00–19.00 Sun ⓜ Metro: Champs-Élysées Clemenceau), which literally means 'Palace of Discovery'. Here, kids can enjoy interactive exhibits including those from astronomy and the earth sciences.

Science-loving children will also enjoy the **Exploradôme** (ⓐ 18 av. Henri Barbusse, pl. du Marché, Vitry-sur-Seine ☎ 01 43 91 16 20 Ⓦ www.exploradome.fr ⏰ 10.30–17.00 Tues, Thur & Fri, 10.30–18.30 Wed & Sat, 13.00–18.30 Sun; school holidays: 10.30–18.30 Mon–Sat, 13.00–18.30 Sun Ⓡ RER C to Vitry-sur-Seine, then bus 180 to pl. de l'Église or ten-min walk). The motto inside this strange-looking brightly coloured building is 'it's forbidden not to touch'. Kids can explore all manner of scientific experiments.

For a good old-fashioned park in the centre of the city, head to the Jardin du Luxembourg (see page 100). With its small-boat

⬥ *Paris is a particularly child-friendly city*

rentals and ornamental pond, puppet theatre and pony rides, this garden is always a good choice to keep children of all ages amused.

The Bois de Vincennes in the 12th *arrondissement* to the east of Paris has a host of attractions for children, including **La Ferme de Paris** (❸ route du Pesage, Bois de Vincennes, 12th ❶ 01 71 28 50 56 ❿ www. paris.fr ❸ 13.30–18.30 Tues–Fri (July, Aug & Easter school holidays); 13.30–17.00 or 18.30 Sat & Sun other times ◉ RER C to Joinville le Pont, then 20-min walk). This 'farm' features several animals and a vegetable garden tended by children. From May/June to mid-September, kids can enjoy *Pestacles* (music festivals for children) in the Bois de Vincennes's Parc Floral. See ❿ www.lespestacles.fr for performance times.

On the west side of Paris in the 16th *arrondissement*, the Bois de Boulogne contains the lovely **Jardin d'Acclimatation** (❶ 01 40 67 90 82 ❿ www.jardindacclimatation.fr ❸ 10.00–18.00 (until 19.00 Apr–Sept) ◉ Metro: Les Sablons or Porte Maillot, then a *petit train* through the woods), with an old-fashioned puppet theatre, miniature train, merry-go-round and small farm.

If you're in Paris at Christmas, take children to **Le Royaume des Neiges** (Kingdom of Snow ❸ Stade Charléty, 99 blvd Kellermann, 13th ❶ 01 44 16 00 00 ❸ 13.30–18.00 Mon–Thur, 13.00–18.00 Sat & Sun (mid–end Dec); last entry 16.30 ◉ RER: Cité Universitaire). The Charléty stadium is transformed into a fun winter resort offering tobogganing, skiing, snowboarding, climbing, a trampoline and much more. The icing on the cake is that it's free!

COMMUNICATIONS

Internet

There is free Internet access in all the main train stations, and cyber cafés are plentiful, especially in the city centre. Most cafés have a large @ in the name. If you need help navigating the French

AZERTY keyboard, staff usually speak some English. A popular chain is called **Milk** (ⓐ Various locations including 53 rue de la Harpe, 5th; 31 blvd Sebastopol, 3rd ☏ 01 44 07 38 89/40 13 06 51 🌐 www.milk lub.com 🕐 24 hrs) because they serve milkshakes; there are several locations throughout Paris.

Another option is using the free Wi-Fi connection offered by the Paris Town Hall available in many public squares from 09.00 to 23.00. Just look for people tapping laptops. Many regular cafés offer this service now, as well as fast-food joints Quick and McDonald's.

Phone

Télécartes (telephone cards) in two sizes (50 units for €8 and 120 units for €15) are on sale at *tabacs* (tobacco stores), newsstands and main metro and RER stations. Public phones are found in post offices, railway and metro stations and in the street, and in some bars and restaurants. They generally take telephone cards and credit cards. All GSM-compatible mobile phones should be usable in France.

International calling rates can be expensive, however, so it may be worth getting a French pay as you go SIM card for your phone. Mobile phone operators are Orange, SFR or Bouygues Telecom. Note that your mobile phone must be 'unlocked' in order for it to accept another SIM card. You could also rent a mobile phone from **Cellhire** (ⓐ 182 av. Charles de Gaulle, Neuilly-sur-Seine ☏ 01 41 43 79 40 🌐 www.cellhire.com) or **Euroteknik** (ⓐ 3 rue Pajou, 16th ☏ 08 20 31 28 12 🌐 www.location-telephone.com).

Post

The French postal service is reliable and efficient. The main post office, located at 52 rue du Louvre, is open 24 hours a day and 365

TELEPHONING FRANCE
To telephone France from abroad, dial the international code first (usually 00), then 33 and the number (skipping the first '0'). Most numbers in France have ten digits and start with 0. In Paris, they start with 01. Mobile phones start with 06 and premium rate numbers start with 08.

TELEPHONING ABROAD
To make an international call from France, dial 00 first, then the country code, followed by the local area code and the number. Country codes are: Australia 61; Canada 1; New Zealand 64; Republic of Ireland 353; South Africa 27; UK 44; US 1.
International operator 118 700 (premium number)
French directory enquiries 118 008

days a year, though service is limited after 19.00. It is the only post office in Europe that never closes. Other post offices are open 08.00–19.00. Monday to Friday and 08.00–12.00 on Saturday.

Stamps are for sale in self-service machines in the post offices as well as *tabacs* (tobacco stores). Postboxes are yellow. At the time of writing, stamps for letters and cards up to 20 grams cost €0.70 within Europe and €0.85 to North America, Australia and New Zealand.

ELECTRICITY

Electricity is 220 volts, 50 Hz, with round-pin wall sockets. UK or non-EU visitors bringing in appliances will need an adaptor, and North Americans will need a transformer as well.

TRAVELLERS WITH DISABILITIES

Anyone with a disability of any sort should first check out the excellent guidebook *Access in Paris*, downloadable chapter by chapter from ⓦ www.accessinparis.org (small donation requested to cover costs). This is detailed, reliable and frequently updated, with research performed mostly by disabled volunteers.

Paris is making a concerted effort to assist those with disabilities. The 'Tourisme & Handicap' label on cultural and leisure sights shows access and facilities for one or more categories of disability. Some restaurants and hotels are also posting the same label. For more information, see the Paris Visitors Bureau website at ⓦ www.parisinfo.com

A number of buses accommodate wheelchairs, and the RER A and metro line 14 have lifts for those with limited mobility. The rest of the metro system is not yet wheelchair-friendly. The RATP (municipal transport system) issues transport network maps that show the bus routes that accommodate wheelchairs. The RER also has special ramps that can be fitted at doorways for wheelchairs. For more information, contact ⓦ http://infomobi.com or call ☏ 08 10 64 64 64

The private association **Compagnons du Voyage** (☏ 01 58 76 08 33 ⓦ www.compagnons.com) provides travel companions and works with the RATP/SNCF to enable travellers with disabilities to be accompanied on the metro, RER, bus and trains (in the whole Île-de-France region). This service currently costs €60 per hour in the Parisian area.

For blind people or the visually impaired, the **AVH** (Association Valentine Haüy ⓐ 5 rue Duroc, 7th ☏ 01 44 49 27 27 ⓦ www.avh.asso.fr) is a good contact.

For information on wheelchair-accessible transport options, try the following companies and associations:

AETAS ☏ 01 39 55 11 11 Ⓦ www.aetas.fr

AIHROP Prices vary, depending on the length of trip. ☏ 01 41 29 01 29

Taxis G7 Horizon Reliable taxi firm with a fleet of cars equipped for wheelchairs. ☏ 01 47 39 00 91 Ⓦ www.taxisg7.fr

TOURIST INFORMATION

Paris Convention and Visitors Bureau, Main Welcome Centre

ⓐ 25 rue des Pyramides, 1st ☏ 08 92 68 30 00 (€0.34/min)
Ⓦ www.parisinfo.com 🕐 09.00–19.00 (May–Oct); 10.00–19.00 (Nov–Apr) Ⓜ Metro: Pyramides

Other welcome centres, with the same telephone number and website, are to be found throughout Paris at the following addresses:

Anvers Welcome Centre ⓐ Facing 72 blvd de Rochechouart, 9th
🕐 10.00–18.00 (except 1 Jan, 1 May & 25 Dec) Ⓜ Metro: Anvers

Expo/Porte de Versailles Welcome Centre ⓐ 1 pl. de la Porte de Versailles, 15th 🕐 11.00–19.00 during trade fairs Ⓜ Metro: Porte de Versailles

Gare de l'Est Welcome Centre ⓐ pl. du 11-Novembre-1918 (by the TGV arrivals), 10th 🕐 08.00–19.00 Mon–Sat Ⓜ Metro: Gare de l'Est

Gare de Lyon Welcome Centre ⓐ 20 blvd Diderot, 12th
🕐 08.00–19.00 Mon–Sat Ⓜ Metro: Gare de Lyon

Gare du Nord Welcome Centre ⓐ 18 rue de Dunkerque, 10th
🕐 08.00–18.00 Ⓜ Metro: Gare du Nord

BACKGROUND READING

Citizens by Simon Schama. Compelling account of how events conspired to cause a ferocious revolution.

The Da Vinci Code by Dan Brown. This mega-selling thriller visits some of Paris's major locations.

The Flaneur: A Stroll through the Paradoxes of Paris by Edmund White. A walking tour of the city in the company of an original mind.

A Moveable Feast by Ernest Hemingway. The story of how Hemingway became a writer is told against a backdrop of 1920s Paris and a cast of legendary characters.

Murder in the Marais by Cara Black. A gripping World War II mystery takes the reader on a tour of the colourful Marais.

Notre Dame de Paris by Victor Hugo. The original story of why Quasimodo got the hump.

Paris: Architecture, History, Art by Ian Littlewood. The best cultural study of the city.

Petite Anglaise by Catherine Sanderson. A personal memoir of an English blogger living in Paris, giving an interesting insight into life in the capital. Her forthright blog caused a media storm in 2006, prompting the book's publication.

Sixty Million Frenchmen Can't Be Wrong by Jean-Benoît Nadeau and Julie Barlow. For once, a non-patronising attempt to identify the essence of what it is to be French.

Emergencies

The following are emergency numbers:

Emergency services ℹ️ 112 (not for car breakdowns)
Pompiers (fire service/first aid) ℹ️ 18
Police ℹ️ 17
SAMU (ambulance service) ℹ️ 15
SOS Médécins (doctors) ℹ️ 01 47 07 77 77
SOS Dentaire (dentists) ℹ️ 01 43 37 51 00
Children's burns ℹ️ 01 44 73 62 54
Adults' burns ℹ️ 01 58 41 26 49/41 41
Poison Treatment Centre ℹ️ 01 40 05 48 48
Sexually transmitted diseases (Bichat Hospital) ℹ️ 01 40 25 84 34

MEDICAL SERVICES

The private **American Hospital** in Paris (📍 63 blvd Victor Hugo, Neuilly-sur-Seine ℹ️ 01 46 41 25 25 🌐 www.american-hospital.org Ⓜ️ Metro: Anatole France or Pont de Levallois-Becon) provides a 24/7 emergency service with bilingual doctors and nurses. If you wish to use your European Health Insurance Card (see page 144), ask at your hotel for the nearest *conventionné* (state-registered) hospital or clinic.

24-hour pharmacy 📍 Les Champs, 84 av. des Champs-Élysées, 8th ℹ️ 01 45 62 02 41 Ⓜ️ Metro: Franklin D. Roosevelt

POLICE

In case of attack or theft, report it to either the nearest police station or *gendarmerie* to where the attack was carried out.

Préfecture de police 📍 9 blvd du Palais, 1st ℹ️ 01 53 71 53 71/40 79 71 57 🌐 www.prefecturedepolice.interieur.gouv.fr Ⓜ️ Metro: Cité

USEFUL PHRASES

Help!	**Fire!**	**Stop!**
Au secours!	Au feu!	Stop!
Ossercoor!	*Oh fur!*	*Stop!*

Call an ambulance/a doctor/the police/the fire service!
Appelez une ambulance/un médecin/la police/les pompiers!
*Ahperleh oon ahngbewlahngss/uhn medesang/lah poleess/
leh pompeeyeh!*

Lost & found office Préfecture de police 📍 36 rue des Morillons, 15th
📞 08 21 00 25 25 🚇 Metro: Convention

EMBASSIES & CONSULATES

Australia 📍 4 rue Jean Rey, 15th 📞 01 40 59 33 00
🚇 Metro: Bir-Hakeim

Canada 📍 35 av. Montaigne, 8th 📞 01 44 43 29 00
🚇 Metro: Alma-Marceau

New Zealand 📍 7 ter rue Léonard de Vinci, 16th 📞 01 45 01 43 43
🚇 Metro: Victor Hugo

Republic of Ireland 📍 4 rue Rude, 16th 📞 01 44 17 67 00
🚇 Metro: Charles de Gaulle-Étoile or Argentine

South Africa 📍 59 quai d'Orsay, 7th 📞 01 53 59 23 23 🚇 Metro: Invalides

UK 📍 35 rue du Faubourg Saint-Honoré, 8th 📞 01 44 51 31 00
🚇 Metro: Madeleine or Concorde

US 📍 2 av. Gabriel, 8th 📞 01 43 12 22 22 🚇 Metro: Champs-Élysées
Clemenceau

A

accommodation 34–9
air travel 48–9, 52,
    140–41
Arc de Triomphe 62, 64
Arènes de Lutèce 104–5
arts *see* culture
Auvers-sur-Oise 122–7

B

background reading
    152–3
bars & clubs 28–31
    see also nightlife
Bastille 80
bicycle hire 32–3, 57, 60
Bois des Vincennes 148
Boulevard
    Saint-Germain 98
bus & coach 56–7, 142

C

cabaret 31
cafés 24–8
    Auvers-sur-Oise 127
    Left Bank 113–15
    Reims 138
    Right Bank East 93–4
    Right Bank West 76–7
canal cruise 82–3
Canal Saint-Martin 83
car hire 60
Catacombes
    de Paris 106, 108
cellar tours (Reims)
    132–3, 135
Centre Pompidou 86
champagne 128, 132–6
Champs-Élysées 64
Château d'Auvers 124
children 146–8
Cimetière du
    Père-Lachaise 83
cinema 9, 31, 58–9, 86,
    88–9 102–3

Cinemathèque
    Française 86
Cité de l'Architecture
    et du Patrimoine 69
Cité Nationale
    de l'Histoire de
    l'Immigration 119–20
Cité des Sciences
    88–9
Conciergerie 64
crime 52–3, 144–5
culture 18–20
customs & duty 143

D

Daubigny,
    Charles-François 126
disabled travellers 151–2
Disneyland 146
driving 52, 60, 122,
    132, 142

E

Église d'Auvers 124
Église Saint-Sulpice 98
Eiffel Tower 106
electricity 150
embassies &
    consulates 155
emergencies 154–5
entertainment 28–31
    see also nightlife
events & festivals 8–11
Exploradôme 147–8

F

fashion 22–3
Ferme de Paris 148
ferry 142
Fondation Cartier 108
food & drink 24–7

G

Galeries Nationales
    du Grand Palais 69
Galerie Nationale
    du Jeu de Paume 67

H

health 144, 154
history 14–15
hot-air ballooning 135
Hôtel des Invalides 100
hotels
    see accommodation

I

Île Saint-Louis 84
Institut du
    Monde Arabe 119
internet 148–9

J

Jardin d'Acclimatation
    148
Jardin du Luxembourg
    44, 100, 148
Jardin des Plantes 102
Jardin des Tuileries 64–5,
    67

L

language 23, 27, 53,
    155, 160
Latin Quarter 103–5
lifestyle 16–17
listings 20, 31
lost property 155
Louvre 70–71

M

Maison de Van Gogh 124
Maison Européenne
    de la Photographie 89
Marais 18, 22, 84
markets 16, 23, 76, 92–3,
    102
metro 56–7
money 143
Montmartre 67–8
multiculturalism 118–19
museums (musées)
    18–20, 31
    d'Art Moderne de
    la Ville de Paris 69–70

des Arts et Metiers 89
de l'Absinthe 125
Carnavalet 44
de la Contrefaçon 20
Dapper 70
Delacroix 108
de l'Erotisme 20
de l'Homme 69
du Louvre 70–71
du Luxembourg 108
Maillol Fondation
  Dina Vierny 109
Marmottan Monet 72
du Montparnasse
  109
de la Musique 90
National des Arts
  Asiatiques-Guimet 72
National d'Histoire
  Naturelle 112
National de
  la Marine 69
de l'Orangerie 67
d'Orsay 109–11
du Quai Branly 111
Rodin 111
Zadkine 111
museum pass 70
music 20, 28–31, 90, 97

N
night views 89, 117, 120
nightlife 28–31
  Left Bank 116–7
  Right Bank East 97
  Right Bank West 79
Notre-Dame (Paris)
  84–5
Notre-Dame (Reims)
  131

O
Odéon 103
opening hours 145
Opéra Bastille 90

Opéra National 72–3
Orsay Museum 109–11

P
Palais des Congrès 20
Palais de la
  Découverte 146–7
Palais Galliera 44
Palais Garnier 72–3
Panthéon 103
Panthéon Bouddhique
  72
Parc des Buttes
  Chaumont 85
Parc de la Villette 85
Paris-Plage 10, 17
Paris in the movies 58–9
Paris Story 46
passports & visas 142–3
Petit Palais 73
phone 149, 150
Place de la Bastille 80
Place de la Concorde 68
Place Delphine 12
Place de la République
  86
Place du Tertre 68
Place Vendôme 13
Place des Vosges 12, 44, 93
police 145, 154
post 149–50
public holidays 11
public transport 48–52,
  56–60

Q
Quartier Latin 103–5

R
rail travel 52, 60, 122,
  130–32, 141
Reims 128–38
restaurants 24–7
  Left Bank 115–16
  Right Bank East 94–6
  Right Bank West 77–8

river cruises 105
rollerblading 33
romance 12–13
Royaume des Neiges
  148

S
Sacré-Coeur 67
safety 52–3, 144–5
Saint-Germain-
  des-Prés 105
Sainte-Chapelle 68
seasons 8
Seine 105
shopping 22–3, 44
  Auvers-sur-Oise 126–7
  Left Bank 112–13
  Reims 136
  Right Bank East
    90–93
  Right Bank West
    73–6
sport 32–3, 68

T
Tenniseum 68
Théâtre National
  de Chaillot 69
time differences 48
toilets 145–6
Tour Eiffel 106
Tour Montparnasse
  106
tourist information 52,
  122, 128, 130, 152
Trocadéro 69

V
Van Gogh, Vincent 122,
  124
vegetarians 26–7
Viaduc des Arts 93
vineyard tours 135–6

W
weather 8, 46

ACKNOWLEDGEMENTS

Thomas Cook Publishing wishes to thank GARRY MARCHANT, to whom the copyright belongs, for the photographs in this book, except for the following images:

BigStockPhoto.com (Galina Barskaya, page 110; Elena Elisseeva, pages 40–41; Mel Gama, page 5; András Sipos, page 74; Marek Slusarczyk, page 7; Sergey Svinarev, page 71; Graça Victoria, page 92); Dreamstime.com (Almir1968, page 104; Eugene Berman, page 140; Dennis Dolkens, page 66; Rene Drouyer, pages 91 & 114; Elena Elisseeva, page 35; Jan Kranendonk, page 96; Philippehalle, page 125; Thaifairs, page 17); Mike Gerrard, page 19; Pierrick Hamonet, page 57; Christopher Holt, page 42; iStockphoto.com (Frédéric de Bailliencourt, page 87; Si Khanh Nguyen, page 65); Julia Peslier, page 13; Alison Rayner, pages 29 & 107; SXC.hu (Christophe Libert, page 101; Jan Tonellato, pages 48–9); World Pictures/Photoshot, page 137.

Send your thoughts to
books@thomascook.com

- Found a great bar, club, shop or must-see sight that we don't feature?
- Like to tip us off about any information that needs a little updating?
- Want to tell us what you love about this handy little guidebook and more importantly how we can make it even handier?

Then here's your chance to tell all! Send us ideas, discoveries and recommendations today and then look out for your valuable input in the next edition of this title.

Email the above address (stating the title) or write to: pocket guides Series Editor, Thomas Cook Publishing, PO Box 227, Coningsby Road, Peterborough PE3 8SB, UK.

WHAT'S IN YOUR GUIDEBOOK?

Independent authors Impartial up-to-date information from our travel experts who meticulously source local knowledge.

Experience Thomas Cook's 165 years in the travel industry and guidebook publishing enriches every word with expertise you can trust.

Travel know-how Thomas Cook has thousands of staff working around the globe, all living and breathing travel.

Editors Travel-publishing professionals, pulling everything together to craft a perfect blend of words, pictures, maps and design.

You, the traveller We deliver a practical, no-nonsense approach to information, geared to how you really use it.

For CAMBRIDGE PUBLISHING MANAGEMENT LIMITED:
Project editor: Karen Beaulah
Layout: Paul Queripel
Proofreaders: Karolin Thomas & Penny Isaac

Useful phrases

English	French	Approx pronunciation
BASICS		
Yes	Oui	Wee
No	Non	Nawng
Please	S'il vous plaît	Sylvooplay
Thank you	Merci	Mehrsee
Hello	Bonjour	Bawngzhoor
Goodbye	Au revoir	Aw revwahr
Excuse me	Excusez-moi	Ekskewzeh-mwah
Sorry	Désolé(e)	Dehzoleh
That's okay	Ça va	Sahr vahr
I don't speak French	Je ne parle pas français	Zher ner pahrl pah frahngsay
Do you speak English?	Parlez-vous anglais?	Pahrlay-voo ohnglay?
Good morning	Bonjour	Bawng-zhoor
Good afternoon	Bonjour	Bawng-zhoor
Good evening	Bonsoir	Bawng-swah
Goodnight	Bonne nuit	Bun nwee
My name is ...	Je m'appelle ...	Zher mahpehl ...
NUMBERS		
One	Un/Une	Uhn/Oon
Two	Deux	Dur
Three	Trois	Trwah
Four	Quatre	Kahtr
Five	Cinq	Sank
Six	Six	Seess
Seven	Sept	Seht
Eight	Huit	Weet
Nine	Neuf	Nurf
Ten	Dix	Deess
Twenty	Vingt	Vang
Fifty	Cinquante	Sangkahnt
One hundred	Cent	Sohn
SIGNS & NOTICES		
Airport	Aéroport	Ahehrohpohr
Rail station	Gare	Gahr
Platform	Quai	Kay
Smoking/	Permit de fumer/	Permee der foom-eh/
No smoking	Interdit de fumer	Anterdee der foom-eh
Toilets	Toilettes	Twahlaitt
Ladies/Gentlemen	Femmes/Hommes	Fam/Ommh
Subway/Bus	Métro/Bus	Maytroa/Booss